With Napoleon's Irish Legion

Miles Byrne in old age

With Napoleon's Irish Legion

The Personal Experiences of an Officer of La Legion Irlandaise During the Napoleonic Wars, 1803-15

ILLUSTRATED

Memoirs of Miles Byrne

Fanny Byrne

LEONAUR

With Napoleon's Irish Legion
The Personal Experiences of an Officer of La Legion Irlandaise During the Napoleonic Wars, 1803-15
Memoirs of Miles Byrne
by Fanny Byrne

ILLUSTRATED

FIRST EDITION

Leonaur is an imprint of Oakpast Ltd

Copyright in this form © 2022 Oakpast Ltd

ISBN: 978-1-915234-64-3 (hardcover)
ISBN: 978-1-915234-65-0 (softcover)

http://www.leonaur.com

Publisher's Notes

Contents

Introduction

In 1798 Miles Byrne was a young and well-to-do farmer at Mona-seed on the northern border of County Wexford. He was a sworn United Irishman, and, before the rebellion actually broke out, was in hiding. From the first raising of the standard, he was active, but his narrative leaves us in doubt by what deeds of bravery he attained to the position of leader; no soldier was ever more modest. After fighting through the whole series of actions, he led a body into the Wicklow hills, where he and his men held out along with Holt and Dwyer till the general dispersal which took place on the news of Humbert's surrender. Byrne made his way to Dublin, and found means to conceal himself and gradually to find occupation in supervising a builder's workmen.

Four years passed by and he had nothing to apprehend; yet when Robert Emmet came to Dublin in the winter of 1802-3, Byrne promptly associated himself in the new peril.

When the rising had failed, Emmet made his way back to Dublin and asked Byrne to carry news to the United Irishmen in Paris. This service of danger was faithfully performed, and the exile found himself among a group of Irishmen, all in the same unhappy situation, yet all hoping for another French invasion in which they should take part. Their hopes ran high when they were formed into the *cadre* or skeleton of a regiment which should be filled up with men when they landed in Ireland, and were sent to be trained on the Breton coast. But months and years passed, and when the Irish Legion was called into service and its ranks filled up, the service was on the Continent.

In the Low Countries, in the Spanish Peninsula, on the Elbe, and on the Rhine, Byrne and his comrades fought for Napoleon, till the great general's star set finally in disaster. Then they—or what was left of them—were dismissed from the French service, for the Bourbons were naturally eager to pleasure the Court of England. Some were actually banished from France; some, more fortunate, had leave to remain on half-pay, and of the latter Byrne was one.

But in 1830 the revolution which dethroned Charles X. brought better days for Miles Byrne. He was not only recalled to full pay, and given the rank of *chef de bataillon* (equivalent to lieutenant-colonel) which had been promised him under Napoleon, but he was at once actively employed, and in the cause of freedom. He held a high command in the first expedition despatched for the liberation of Greece.

For many years after this he was an ordinary regimental officer in the French Army; these *Memoirs* were the occupation of his leisure after he had finally retired, and the latter part of them was clearly never finished. The book, as it originally appeared, was edited by Mrs. Byrne, and it made three volumes, of which the first was occupied with the description of his experiences of rebellion in Ireland, while the second gave an admirable narrative of his campaigns under Buonaparte, including the whole history of Napoleon's Irish Legion from its formation to its dissolution. These two volumes are evidently as their author intended them to be. The third is little more than loose leaves from a notebook but a notebook full of interesting material. Opening with an account of Byrne's own life in Paris before the formation of the Legion, it passes into a general characterisation of the Irish exiles then in France. The account of the Greek campaign is fragmentary; and there is a good deal of repetition and defective arrangement

Care has been taken to leave in full Byrne's judgment on the men with whom he served or whom he met during his residence in Paris; for nothing is more remarkable in the book than the clearness and justice of perception which these judgments display. Byrne's mind was neither subtle nor brilliant; but it was evidently rich in common sense, and it combined generosity with a rigorous conception of honour and principle.

As a soldier, he seems to have been the very type of a regimental officer, whose place is in the fighting line, whose concern is not with the general conduct of a campaign or an action, but who can be trusted to act boldly, decisively and intelligently in the individual circumstances of war. His book throughout makes one feel the most agreeable and most human aspect of warfare—the generous relations between man and man, the cordiality of comradeship, the interludes of gaiety and good-humoured pleasure—better than any other known to me except the admirable autobiography which General Sir George Napier wrote, to tell his children how he and his brothers and their brothers in arms fought in the Peninsula "for fun and glory."

But there one strikes a contrast and a sad one. Byrne was not, like the Napiers, a soldier by choice; necessity and unjust dominion drove him from his farm. He and his comrades were the descendants of the Wild Geese—"war-dogs battered in every clime," fighters in every cause but their own. His book gives an extraordinary picture of the dispersion of his race: Irish names figure in it under every flag in Europe. And the book is naturally pervaded from first to last with a fierce resentment, the exile's anger against those who keep him from his home, against those who hold his native country in subjection. Byrne and his comrades fight for France against England with more than a Frenchman's detestation of the enemy. Is this to be wondered at?

Stephen Gwynn.

This Leonaur edition focuses entirely on Byrne's service in the Irish Legion until the unit's disbanding after the fall of Napoleon.

MILES BYRNE
1843

From a drawing by Mrs Byrne
Etched by Mr A.J. Holroyd

CHAPTER 1

Formation of Irish Legion

At the end of November, 1803, our excitement was greater than ever, thinking of scarcely anything except the study of military tactics, and expecting hourly to receive our brevets. I had bought, when I arrived at Paris, the *réglement* or *ordonnance* on the exercise and manoeuvres of infantry, and I began to know tolerably well the theory; and as I had some practice in Ireland in fighting against regular troops, I felt satisfied I could make my way like other officers.

At length the First Consul's decree appeared to have an Irish Legion in the service of France organised, to be composed of infantry regiments, with artillery and cavalry attached to it. This Legion was to be completed on landing in Ireland, to twenty-five thousand men. Our commissions or brevets of officers in the service of France, were dated the 7th of December, 1803, and on receiving them, we had orders to march to Morlaix.

We were to go by regular *étapes*, or day's marches, or if we wished we might take the coaches, and the distance being 148 leagues, we had twenty-one days to make the journey. Hugh Ware and I decided to make it on foot, as we should be the better prepared for campaigning after such a long march in winter. Those officers who had money to pay their places in the coach, could spend fifteen days more with their friends at Paris, and arrive at Morlaix the day fixed by the "*feuille de route*," or military order of march.

One day Mr. Thomas Addis Emmet read me a letter he had just received (at Paris) from William Dowdall, stating that he and John Allen, and a young man of the name of Sandy Devereux, had escaped safely to Cadiz, after many risks and perils. He asked me questions about Devereux. "As to Allen and Dowdall," he said, "I know them sufficiently myself to answer for them."

I told him that Devereux was one of our hurling associates at Donnybrook Green, that he was from the County of Wexford, and employed in the mercantile firm of Cornelius O'Loughlan and Company in Dublin, that I did not think he was committed in our unfortunate affairs.

"No, but you see by this letter that he has acted a noble part." Young Devereux took out a passport for himself to go to transact business at Cadiz for his employers. He went and left this passport with Allen and Dowdall where they were hiding, that they might endeavour to make out others for themselves, and to imitate it as nearly as possible. He requested them to have a similar one to theirs made for him, as he would destroy the original passport, lest it might be the means of discovering the false ones, and that he would take his chance with them through thick and thin.

A Mr. Cummings, who had been one of the State prisoners in Dublin, when he was allowed to expatriate himself, went to Cadiz to practise there as a physician. He wrote to Mr. Emmet to pray him to obtain for him a commission in the Irish regiment in order that he might be of the expedition destined for Ireland.

A Mr. O'Kelly, an officer of one of the Irish regiments in the Spanish service, being at Cadiz when Allen and Dowdall arrived there, wrote also to Mr. Emmet that he wished to make part of the French Army to be sent to obtain the independence of his native country.

Mr. Emmet gave the names of these five gentlemen to the Minister of War, recommending them as true Irish patriots, and immediately commissions of sub-lieutenants were sent to Cadiz for John Allen, William Dowdall, Sandy Devereux, Dr. Cummings and O'Kelly, with orders for them to repair forthwith to Morlaix, where the Irish Legion was assembled.

It being remarked that whilst many of the distinguished and meritorious Irish patriots got only the rank of ensigns and lieutenants, others with very inferior claims, got that of captain, the highest then given; Mr. Emmet remonstrated with the Minister of War, Berthier, who promised him that Adjutant-General MacSheehy, charged with the organisation of the Legion, should have precise instructions at Morlaix, to report to the War Office on the subject, and that he might rest satisfied the injustice should be repaired, as soon as MacSheehy's report was received.

Some of the injustice was remedied, though not for a month or two later. William Barker, Pat MacCanna, Pat Gallagher, Valentine Derry, Augustin O'Meally, John Sweeny, Hugh Ware, and William Dowdall

The flag of the Irish Legion

received their commissions as captains, and several *sous*-lieutenants received theirs of lieutenants at the same time.

Previous to our leaving Paris for the coast, a young man arrived from Dublin, Terence O'Reilly; he was the bearer of a letter of introduction from a Dr. Sheridan to Dr. MacNeven; the latter had just time to present him to General Dalton, before quitting Paris for Morlaix, and as O'Reilly spoke French well, he got on better than others at the War Office. He got his commission of lieutenant in the month of January, 1804, and joined the Irish Legion at Morlaix.

I am persuaded that he did not consider it a triumph to have obtained a higher rank, and to be placed over so many of his countrymen, such as the following: Paul Murray, Edmond Saint-Leger, Joseph Parrott, William Dowdall, John Allen, and many others, who had only the rank of *sous*-lieutenants at the time. However, O'Reilly's advancement afterwards was slow indeed. It was only after the siege of Flushing in 1809, where he distinguished himself in the Irish battalion there, fighting against the English, that he was recompensed with the cross of the Legion of Honour, and later he was named captain in the 1st battalion of the Irish regiment, then in garrison at Landau, near the Rhine, in 1810.

In the campaigns of 1813 and 1814, O'Reilly served with distinction, and he had the good fortune to get his brevet of *chef de bataillon* before Napoleon's abdication in 1814. After the Restoration of the Bourbons, and the battle of Waterloo, Commandant O'Reilly retired to Evreux, where he finished his days. I have often had to mention him in my notes on our campaigns, and I trust I may be excused now for this anticipation. I esteemed O'Reilly as a brave and an honourable officer, and I liked him as an obliging, good comrade, and I cannot forget that he was one of those that expressed regret that I had not obtained my commission of Napoleon of superior officer before the downfall of Napoleon.

Not being encumbered with much luggage, my effects were soon packed up, and I had nothing to buy, for every article for the equipment of the officers had been sent to the depot of the Irish Legion at Morlaix. Amongst them was a quantity of superfine dark green cloth, sufficient for the uniforms of 150 officers, and as our master tailor had at his disposition all the tailors of Augereau's army, a short time would suffice to have then made up. The officers were advised to have small portmanteaus, not weighing more than fourteen pounds, which they could easily carry under their arm, going on board the fleet at

Brest, and also on landing on the coast of Ireland, when they would answer as pillows at the bivouac. I had one of this description already, which held my two shirts, stockings, slippers, etc., so I had not to buy a portmanteau. Having now all things settled ready to set out on my march, save to pay my farewell visits to those dear friends whom I soon expected to have the happiness of meeting in Ireland. Alas! my expectations were not realised.

My first visit was to Mr. Thomas Addis Emmet and his amiable lady, his son Robert, with his two little sisters, one of them born in the prison of Dublin, and the other in that of Fort George in Scotland. Mr. Emmet kindly enquired of me about my money matters, saying that he had received another remittance of sixty pounds from that generous, worthy Irish patriot, Lord Cloncurry, to be distributed amongst the Irish refugees who might stand in need of money. I had to show him a few half-guineas I had still remaining, to convince him that I had sufficient with my *feuille de route* money, to make the journey to Morlaix, and I told him I owed nothing, etc.

He opened a trunk to show me two bags of silver, containing Lord Cloncurry's remittance, which he had just brought from the bankers. Mr. Emmet paid me some compliments on the saving way I had lived, and then we embraced and separated, alas! forever. His son Robert, about nine or ten years old was waiting in the outer room. He took the small cord or chain from his watch, and asked me to keep it for his sake, which I did carefully until 1813, when my baggage fell into the hands of the enemy on the Bober.

Amongst the wives and daughters of the other Irish exiles of whom I had to take leave before starting for the coast in December, 1803, was Mrs. Tone, with her three children, two boys and a girl. The latter was a fine grown girl of twelve or fourteen; she had the misfortune to lose her and one of her sons at Paris sometime after. Fortunately, her other son lived to publish his heroic father's admirable *Memoirs*, which prove to the world that Ireland would have been a free country, governing herself, had the General-in-Chief, Hoche, been on board the same vessel as Theobald Wolfe Tone, in the Bay of Bantry, on Christmas Day, 1796.

Mrs. Tone was in every respect worthy of being the companion of her lamented husband. She was very well mannered and very obliging to her friends. I recollect in 1806, when our regiment was on march to Mayence, that Captain Barker had to leave his son Arthur, then nine years of age, with Mrs. Tone, who kindly kept him nearly a month with her own children, till he was placed in the Irish College, where he finished his education in 1815. Mr. and Mrs. Barker were ever grateful to Mrs. Tone for her kindness on this occasion; and indeed, their son, Mr. Arthur Barker, though so young then, remembers being the playmate of Tone's children as an event not to be forgotten.

Though Mrs. Jackson, the widow of the Reverend W. Jackson, one of the first martyrs to the independence of his native land, had but a small pension to live on, still she had her son and daughter very well educated. Mrs. Jackson was clever and well-informed, and her children availed themselves of this advantage. They were clever and sprightly. Miss Jackson was married to a merchant at Havre. In 1820, Mr. Warden and I signed a paper for her to obtain a passport for Italy, where she went to visit her mother and brother, who were residing at Leghorn.

Of all the exiled Irish ladies in Paris in 1803, poor Mrs. Hamilton was the most to be pitied; she had heard of the melancholy end, the trial and execution, of her beloved uncle, Thomas Russell, on whom she doated, and every hour she feared she would hear that her husband had shared the same fate, a reward being offered for his apprehension. It appeared impossible for him to procure a safe hiding-place, or the means of escaping from a country where terror of every description was reigning, with martial law and all its horrors. However, William Hamilton was not sold and betrayed into the hands of his enemies, as was the unfortunate Russell.

To finish my visits, I had still to call on Messrs. John Sweetman, Mat Bowling, Richard MacCormick, Edward Lewins, Delany, Dr. Mac-Mahon, etc. These patriots were stopping at Paris, hoping they might soon be called on to co-operate in their civil capacity with us, once we were landed in Ireland. Poor Arthur MacMahon had an attack of paralysis the day before I left Paris. My friend and former comrade, Paul Murray, not feeling the same activity and power of marching that he had when we were together in the Wicklow mountains in 1798, set off for Morlaix on foot, the day after he received his commission, intending to take the coach occasionally, when tired with walking.

Hugh Ware and I agreed to set out on foot and to march the whole way to Morlaix, without incurring the expense of either horse or coach-hire. He came to sleep at my lodgings in the Rue de la Harpe, the night before we set off: he having had to give up the hired furniture he had at his own lodgings. At break of day, we took our little portmanteaus under our arms and brought them to Mr. William Law-

Irish Legion uniforms

less's apartment in the Rue de la Loi (Rue de Richelieu); he kindly promised to bring them, with his own baggage, by the coach to Morlaix. He told us that he, MacNeven, Sweeny, Tennant, Gallagher, and Lacy had retained the six inside places of the diligence, or stage coach, leaving Paris for Morlaix ten days after, and we might be sure of our portmanteaus on arriving there.

We then took leave of Captain Lawless, who was still in bed, and we marched off to Versailles, where Ware had given a rendezvous to his cousin Joseph Parrott, Captain Maguire, Lambert, John Reilly, Fitzpatrick, and James MacEgan, a lad of fourteen years of age. After we had breakfasted and visited the *château*, waited to see the famous clock strike, and the cock turn out and flutter its wings—the only remaining fixture in this once renowned palace, the scene of intrigue, debauchery and artificial greatness—we set out again, to make another *étape* (or day's march and halt) on the road to Rambouillet, where we got billets of lodging and passed the night.

Hugh Ware being an admirer of country scenery, a judge of land and of architecture, (it appears from the State Papers that Ware was a land surveyor by profession), well read and versed in history, it was a great advantage to me to have him as my fellow-traveller. He would wish to examine every mansion or *château* near the road, and tell us something of their antiquity or renown. That part of Normandy through which we passed to Alençon, was rich and well cultivated. One night it blew a terrible storm. Next morning, we found on our march the road in many places strewed with fine trees, torn from their roots by this whirlwind.

We said, what a pity that the expedition was not ready at Brest, as the English Fleet must now be off to Torbay, from its blockading station before Brest. It was after such a storm that General Hoche's Fleet sailed with his expedition in 1796 for Ireland, and passing at Rennes, it brought to our recollection that he had his headquarters in that town previous to embarking, and that it was there that he got the proclamation translated and printed in the Portuguese language, by a priest of that nation, in order to baffle the English spies, who thought in consequence that Hoche's expedition was destined for Portugal.

This part of Brittany through which we were passing reminded us of our own country; the climate nearly the same, fine pasturage to be seen on every side, the cattle generally of an inferior race, cultivation much neglected, and the poor people only beginning to recover from the bad effects of their civil wars. However, our journey continued to the end to be agreeable, indeed; marching four or five leagues before breakfast, and six or seven again before we reached the town where we passed the night; and though in the month of December, we had time to take a view of the churches, or anything curious, before going to dinner. We remarked that the country people returning from their fairs and markets, generally had taken a hearty glass of cider brandy, and their dresses were quite different as we approached Morlaix. We arrived at this town after a long day's march, late at night, and next morning paid our visits.

We had the satisfaction of again meeting many of our friends. Lawless, MacNeven, and the other officers who travelled by the coach, only arrived the day before us. We got billets of lodging. Mine was with a Mr. Premcour, a receiver of contributions, by whom I was most graciously received. I had invitations from this gentleman and his lady to evening parties, which was a great advantage to me in learning French.

My valued friend Val Derry had arranged for our mess at the Hotel de France, where we had an excellent table, and in the best part of the town, near the bridge, on the quay. Mr. and Mrs. Barker lived next door, and Thomas Markey was just arrived from Bordeaux. He gave us a splendid account of General Augereau's army, with which he had been on the frontiers of Spain. It was now assembled in the neighbourhood of Brest, ready to embark for Ireland. The adjutant-general, MacSheehy, who was charged with the organisation of the Legion, accompanied us to the magazine, where we received our swords, epaulettes, etc., and he gave orders to the master tailor and bootmaker respecting our uniforms.

Five days after, I had mine, and I was completely equipped and ready to embark. General MacSheehy was exceedingly busy receiving the officers who were arriving every day and by every stage coach from all parts of France, and giving his orders to have them equipped forthwith, ready to embark. We were truly glad to see Allen, Dowdall, Sandy Devereux, Cummings and O'Kelly arriving after their long journey from Cadiz. Allen and Dowdall's escape was fortunate indeed, for the state of Ireland was such at the time they were hiding in the neighbourhood of Dublin, that it was thought impossible for them to procure means of getting away.

Morlaix was the rendezvous of the Irish exiles in January, 1804. Mr. and Mrs. Barker met amongst them many of their former friends, and I recollect spending a most agreeable day at their house, when they entertained at dinner a number of the officers, such as Adjutant-General MacSheehy, MacNeven, Lawless, William O'Meara, Mandeville, Masterson, O'Gorman, Derry, Fitzhenry, etc. Captain Barker seemed quite happy to have at his table that day officers who had been in the Irish Brigade before 1792, and others who were by his side at the Battle of Vinegar Hill on the 21st of June, 1798, where he lost his arm fighting for Ireland's rights. Our evenings were spent agreeably enough, and our morning occupations were highly amusing; learning the positions of a soldier without arms, marching in quick and ordinary time; learning the manual exercise with the musket, etc. We had the best French instructors, who told us we should in a short time be capable of becoming instructors ourselves to teach others.

Unfortunately, Adjutant-General MacSheehy, notwithstanding his great activity and talents as a staff-officer, was not equal to the task of organising a political corps like the Irish Legion, composed of patriots, all of whom had suffered in their country's cause, but differing on many points as to the best way of redressing her grievances. He was young, and wanted experience in Irish matters.

CHAPTER 2

Movements of Irish Legion

The Irish patriots, disappointed by General Hoche not landing in December, 1796, as they expected, were driven into partial insurrection by the persecution of the English Government, which was irritated at their attempt to throw off its yoke, and at their calling in the aid of France.

The general rising that was intended in 1798, after the system of the United Irishmen had been organised, failed in consequence of Lord Edward Fitzgerald and several other leading men being betrayed and arrested. However, three or four counties made great efforts, *viz.*: Kildare, Wicklow, Carlow and Wexford. The latter county alone occupied the English forces, and was successful in many engagements. Had General Humbert landed with his eleven hundred men in the month of June, 1798, whilst the people of Wexford were in full force, instead of August, 1798, when they were dispersed and discouraged, every county in Ireland would have taken up arms, as they only wanted a rallying point, and their independence would have been immediately proclaimed, and consequently, everything like an English faction, or vestige of government, would have been obliged to surrender.

Though General Humbert arrived too late and only when the spirits of the Irish patriots were much broken, still as he advanced into the country, he found the people everywhere ready to join him—but they were unarmed, and he had not brought the arms that were promised. He capitulated to Lord Cornwallis, who was at the head of a force of more than thirty thousand men, leaving the unfortunate Irish to their fate, who were butchered by the soldiery for several days throughout the country.

In 1803, as soon as hostilities commenced between France and England, and after the short Peace of Amiens, the patriotic Irish, who wished for the independence of their country, began to hope for assistance from France, as General Buonaparte, on whose aid they could reckon, was at the head of the government as First Consul.

Many of those exiled Irish were at this time in different parts of France, and particularly at Paris. They chose Mr. Thomas Addis Emmet as their agent or representative to the First Consul, who consulted with him and Mr. Arthur O'Connor on the matter. They informed him that the Irish patriots in France were ready to go as volunteers in any expedition which had for its object the emancipation of their country.

Although Robert Emmet's plan and preparations for the organisation of Ireland became known to the English Government after the explosion of the depot in Patrick-street, Dublin, and the final fate of this ever-to-be-lamented martyr, yet all tended to shew the First Consul the great resources of the Irish patriots, and he eagerly entered into all the details related in the report on the state of Ireland, given to him by Mr. Thomas Addis Emmet on the arrival at Paris of the confidential agent sent from Dublin in August, 1803; and, in consequence, it was stipulated that a French Army should be sent to assist the Irish to get rid of the English yoke.

And the First Consul understanding from Mr. Emmet that Augereau was a favourite with the Irish nation, had him appointed general-in-chief to command the expedition; and immediately ordered the formation of an Irish legion in the service of France. He gave to all those gentlemen who volunteered to enter the Irish legion commissions as French officers, so that in the event of their falling into the hands of the English they should be protected; or, should any violence be offered them, he should have the right to retaliate on the English prisoners in France.

The decree of the First Consul for the formation of this Irish legion was dated November, 1803; by it, the officers were all to be Irishmen, or Irishmen's sons born in France. The pay was to be the same as that given to officers and soldiers of the line of the French Army. No rank was to be given higher than captain till they should land with the expedition in Ireland.

There were two exceptions. Captain Blackwell, whose long services and campaigns with the French Armies entitled him to promotion, received his commission as *chef de bataillon* to the Irish Legion.

The second was Arthur O'Connor, whose renown began when he was High Sheriff of the county of Cork, and who, when a member of the Irish House of Commons, made the ablest speech in favour of

Catholic Emancipation that ever was pronounced in the Irish Parliament, and who, immediately after this speech, retired from Parliament, accepting the Chiltern Hundreds. He was the friend and companion of Lord Edward Fitzgerald; the delegate to General Hoche; the disinherited nephew of the Tory Lord Longueville; the prisoner tried at Maidstone, a trial which attracted the attention of the nobility; the "long imprisoned" in the jail of Dublin, and at Fort George in Scotland.

He received his commission as general-of-division in the service of France, dated the 24th of February, 1804, with orders to repair to Brest to make part of the General-in-Chief Augereau's staff, composed of many officers of great distinction, such as Lamarque (who had then the rank of *chef d'escadron*, or lieutenant-colonel, and afterwards was the great General Lamarque who took Capri in 1808 and pacified La Vendée in the Hundred Days of 1815), and General Donzelot, chief of the staff, highly talented. The three generals who had the command of the divisions under Augereau were men of the greatest military experience: Generals Mathieu Dumas, De Jardin, and the enterprising General Bonnet, so much distinguished in Spain.

It was, however, stipulated that, on leaving Brest, a certain number of captains were to get the rank of colonel, and also a certain number of lieutenants that of lieutenant-colonel; which rank was to be confirmed to them even in the event of the expedition failing and their getting back to France. In naming these captains and lieutenants, the preference was to be given to those who had been obliged to expatriate themselves for their exertions in Ireland to effect its independence.

Adjutant-General MacSheehy, an Irishman by birth, but in the French service, was charged with the organisation of the legion, and for that purpose was commanded to repair to Morlaix, where the Irish exiles were assembled. He received unlimited powers at Morlaix to propose officers for advancement up to the rank of captain; all he named were confirmed by the Minister of War, General Berthier.

The greatest exertions were made to have the officers splendidly equipped and ready for sailing. They received the same outfit given to French officers entering on campaign; no expense being spared by the French Government. The best French instructors, both for the infantry and artillery, were sent to teach the officers the French military tactics, and when the legion was reviewed at Brest by Marshal Augereau, previous to their intended embarkation, he put a French regiment under their orders, and made each officer command in turn. He was much pleased with their knowledge of manoeuvring the infantry, and also with the way they exercised the artillery. He found the officers capable of instructing companies of artillery on arriving in Ireland. On this occasion, each officer received 400 *francs* more in addition to his outfit, or what is called in French, "*une gratification extraordinaire d'entrée en campagne.*" This gratification of 400 *francs* was given to every officer afterwards who entered the Irish legion—a favour granted to no other regiment.

★★★★★★★★★★

After Marshal Augereau's review and inspection of the Irish legion at Brest in 1804, we went in the evening to the military coffee house, which was very crowded, with naval officers, as well as those of the army. Our officers wondered much to see a lieutenant of one of the ships of war, coming to the table where we were taking our coffee and shake hands with me. He was the officer who had been ordered by the commodore to escort me up the river to Bordeaux in 1803, when I escaped from Ireland, and who treated me so well during the night I spent on the passage, in his little war-sloop. He had made great progress in speaking English, taking lessons, he said, every day, from my countryman Brown, of Baggot Street, Dublin, who was a sailor on board the commodore's vessel, and who had been so useful to me also. He told me that Brown had got promotion and was then on board one of the admiral's vessels as interpreter, and that he was a well behaved, sober man, which I was very glad to learn, as sailors in general are too apt to take a hearty glass. I regretted not having more chat with this young officer who had been so kind to me at Bordeaux; but we had to separate; he to return to sleep on board his vessel, I to go to my lodgings and prepare to march back to Carhaix in the morning.

★★★★★★★★★★

The legion assembled at Morlaix was marched to Quimper in March, 1804, where all these officers who had been proposed for advancement by Adjutant-General MacSheehy received their brevets. From Quimper the legion was ordered to Carhaix, in Finistère, a small town (the native place of Latour d'Auvergne, "*premier grenadier de France*"), which from being more inland and less frequented, was better suited for manoeuvring, and where the best results were obtained. Two officers, Captain Tennant and Captain William Corbet, were deputed from thence by the legion to go to Paris to be present at the coronation of the emperor (May, 1804), who on that occasion presented it, as well as the French regiments, with colours and an eagle. On one side of the colours was written "*Napoleon I, empereur des Français, à la legion irlandaise,*" and on the reverse was, a harp (without a crown), with the inscription: "*L'indépendance d'Irlande*."

The Irish legion was the only foreign corps in the French service to whom Napoleon ever entrusted an eagle.

Rejoicings took place at Carhaix, as in the other towns of France, in honour of the coronation, by order of the authorities; and an unhappy dispute took place there between two officers of the legion, Captain Sweeny and Captain Thomas Corbet, which disagreement ended in a duel after the legion marched to Lesneven. (The cause of this duel was that General MacSheehy told Sweeny that Corbet had accused him—Sweeny—of omitting to raise his hand in assent during the ceremony of swearing allegiance on this occasion—S. G). They fought with pistols; both were wounded, but Captain Corbet died of his wounds the same night.

When Marshal Augereau, who commanded the army at Brest, heard of the dispute, he ordered the chief of his staff, General Donzelot, with Lieutenant-General O'Connor, to repair to Carhaix to inspect the Irish legion; and in consequence of their report, it was ordered in August, 1804, to Lesneven, where the command of the legion was taken from Adjutant-General MacSheehy. Unfortunately for the Irish officers, he proved himself quite unfit to remain at their head. He was capricious, passionate and vindictive; consequently, not impartial as a chief should be. One instance which I shall relate will suffice to show how he used, or abused, the confidence with which the war minister intrusted him.

Being at exercise one day at Carhaix, the Adjutant-Major, Caugnan, made use of some expression which displeased Captain O'Malley. The latter, when the exercise finished, asked the adjutant-major, who, though a Frenchman, knew English well, if he would apologise to him for the expression, "You are a *bête*, stupid, etc.," which he had used during the manoeuvres. He replied he had no apology to offer. Captain O'Malley then told him he was a coward, and unworthy to be admitted amongst gentlemen, etc.

Though O'Malley might not be as expert as other officers in the manoeuvres, none could surpass him in his knowledge of the etiquette of duelling; his native land of Connaught never produced a cooler, nor a braver, nor a more honourable antagonist than he was; and on the ground, his amiable manners and daring courage were the wonder of the seconds, and furnished a theme of gay conversation. He gloried in the part he had taken with General Humbert in Ireland in 1798; and the great sacrifices his family suffered and went through, in the loss of property of every kind, were his pride.

Adjutant-General MacSheehy, as soon as he heard the Adjutant-Major Caugnan's complaint against O'Meally, told him at once he should challenge him, and he sent for Captain William O'Mara and bid him be second to Caugnan. Captain Ware was O'Malley's second. They fought with pistols; the adjutant-major was wounded, and Captain O'Malley was put into the town prison, and next morning he was escorted by *gendarmes* to the *château* of Brest, to which prison he was condemned for fifteen days, by the chief who ordered the duel!

How far was I from thinking that this duel would retard my military career! Being with several officers in the street when the *gendarmes* were conducting O'Malley to prison, I said, if he had been wounded, Caugnan would no doubt have been put into prison, but as they fought honourably, it was strange that there should be any question of imprisonment. Captain Pat MacSheehy, the general's cousin, went and told him that I was speaking against him. On which he took and tore in pieces a proposition he had made to the Minister of War for my commission of captain, and which I should have received in eight days, instead of years, which I had to wait ere I obtained that rank.

But MacSheehy seemed to care very little about the martyrs who had suffered for Ireland. Commandant Blackwell was deprived of his rank for some time, in consequence of MacSheehy's reports against him to the War Office. They both quit the legion at Lesneven in 1804, and were soon afterwards employed in the Grand Army. But they were not soon forgotten by their countrymen, who had to remain in the legion and to suffer from having had chiefs so incapable of commanding even respect for themselves.

Captain Sweeny resigned when his wound got well, and retired to Morlaix, where he married a relation of General Moreau. Captain MacNeven gave in his resignation and went to New York, America. Captain Gallagher resigned and went to reside at Bordeaux.

The legion being at Lesneven, M. Peterzelli, a *chef de bataillon* of the 16th regiment *léger*, was appointed provisionally to the command of the Irish legion, under the control of General Harty, who was ordered to Landernau, where a part of the legion was sent from Lesneven to be under his command, waiting for the expedition that was expected to sail for Ireland. He was an Irishman by birth, and had acquired a military reputation for his brave and decided conduct in preventing Berwick's regiment, in garrison at Landau in 1792, from marching across the Rhine to join the enemy's camp at the other side.

Harty was captain of the grenadiers' company, and seeing the regiment marching on the direction of the Rhine, he asked his Lieutenant-Colonel, O'Mahony, where he intended going to? The answer was, "To join our princes on the other side." Captain Harty said he would not desert the country he had adopted. He harangued the regiment and returned with it to Landau, leaving Lieutenant-Colonel O'Mahony and three officers who followed him to go away and cross the Rhine to the enemy's camp. Harty received the grateful thanks of the governor and the inhabitants of Landau, when he returned there triumphantly at the head of Berwick's regiment, which he had saved from the foul crime of desertion to the enemy with arms and baggage.

These antecedents, and what I knew of General Harty's patriotism and great desire to see Ireland independent, his private and public character as a man of honour and a brave soldier, made me glad to be of the detachment of Landernau, where he commanded; besides, several of the officers who composed it were my best friends and comrades, such as Captains Ware, Barker, Fitzhenry, Masterson, Saint-Leger, Murray, MacMahon, etc. We were happy and united, and rejoiced much to be under General Harty's orders; nearer to Brest than we were at Lesneven. From a little hill just over Landernau, we could see the masts of the ships in the bay of Brest, from whence we expected soon to sail with an army to liberate our beloved country; this view caused sensations that exiles alone can feel and appreciate.

General Harty being himself an infantry officer, kept us busily employed at exercise and studying the evolutions and tactics of that arm. He had some officers to dine with him every day, and did the honours of his rank and command in the most agreeable manner to them.

Eight Irishmen, soldiers in an English regiment at Jersey, escaped in a boat to the French coast, and were sent to the legion. They told General Harty that they had heard of the Irish legion in the French service, and that all their countrymen in the English regiments were disposed to do as they had done, whenever an opportunity was offered, etc. They were very well-behaved men for English soldiers. One of them being from the county of Kilkenny, gave General Harty news about many of his friends there.

The Generals Fontaine and Sarazan, who had been with Humbert in Ireland, were attached to Marshal Augereau's staff, waiting to accompany the expedition. General Sarazan was not liked by the generals. It was said of him that he had written reports against them to the emperor. It would appear he was capable of doing bad things; for, in

1813, he had a command at Boulogne-sur-Mer, when he deserted to an English frigate off the coast, and it was suspected that he had been in the pay of England from the time of General Humbert's capitulation in 1798. At the passage of the prisoners through Dublin he was allowed to walk about the city on parole, whilst Humbert and the other French officers were in prison. After the restoration of the Bourbons, General Sarazan came back to France, and, some time after, he was tried and condemned to the galleys for bigamy.

In the spring of 1805, the detachment at Landernau was ordered to rejoin the legion at Lesneven, and although this latter town had a choice society, in which the officers were well received, we who were of the detachment regretted leaving Landernau, where we had spent our time so profitably and agreeably. However, we were well received and on the most friendly terms with the inhabitants of Lesneven; concerts were organised by the officers, who played on different instruments, with the young men of the town who were musicians. Captain Lawless and the two Saint-Legers arranged those musical meetings.

At a ball given by the officers of the legion, I was appointed one of the stewards, and I had the mission of being bearer of the invitations to the society of Landernau, which flattered me very much. Captain Markey accompanied me, and we spent a pleasant day amongst our acquaintances there; indeed, our time passed cheerfully enough at Lesneven. We used sometimes to hire horses and ride to Brest, to visit our friend Captain Murphy, who was on board the admiral's vessel, as head pilot of the fleet, with the rank of captain of a frigate. From him we learned that all the preparations were completed, and on a vast scale, for the expedition: twenty-one ships of the line, with frigates and transport vessels sufficient to carry twenty-five thousand troops, artillery, arms, etc.

We always returned in high spirits and full of hope to our garrison after our visit to Captain Murphy at Brest. He was much respected there by the officers of the fleet: his reputation as the bearer of General Humbert's despatches to the French Government in 1798 was well known, and he had been presented with pistols of honour by the Directory for his brilliant conduct on the occasion.

Captain Pat MacSheehy had a dispute with the mayor's son of Lesneven, young Carranda; after firing their pistols the mayor's son wanted to fight with swords; the seconds prevailed and settled the matter. Unfortunately, the mayor's son, on returning to town, said to some of his friends, whom he met, "Those Irish officers won't fight but with pistols."

Lieutenant Osmond happening to be present, said to him, "I am one of those Irish officers, and I am ready to prove to you the contrary."

They went to the field and fought with small swords. The mayor's son received a desperate wound, and was carried, in what appeared a dying state to his father's house. This caused a painful sensation. An order came in the night from the general-in-chief at Brest, for the legion to quit Lesneven forthwith and march to Quimper. Thus, by the folly of a half-crazy fellow, like Pat MacSheehy, were the officers obliged to take leave of a charming society, in which they had spent more than a year most agreeably. To be sure, they were not likely to lose by a change of garrison. Quimper being the chief town of the department, greater advantages in every way were to be had there; a very choice society, composed of many elegant and handsome ladies of the ancient families in that country, frequented the balls and evening entertainments given by the *prefet* of Finistère, M. Miolis, brother to the general who acquired such notoriety afterwards at Rome, by the arrest of Pope Pius VII.

In the beginning of the summer of 1805, General Harty was named inspector-general, and ordered to Quimper, to inspect the Irish legion. This inspection cheered the spirits of the officers and made them still hope that the expedition would soon sail, to free their country from the foreign yoke.

Jerome Buonaparte, on his way to Brest, passed by Quimper. He stopped at the *prefet's* hotel a short time. Lieutenant Saint-Leger and thirty men were on guard there: he sent them away, saying, that a captain of a vessel was not entitled to a guard of honour; he thanked Saint-Leger, and begged him to leave one of his sergeants as platoon or orderly at his disposition while he remained.

A few days after, we learned that Jerome Buonaparte and a part of the French fleet had sailed from Brest, which omened badly for poor Ireland; indeed, from that moment we could see plainly that there were little hopes of anything being done, till the fleet was again re-united.

Captain Derry resigned, to go to America; those officers who were determined to remain in the French service, to learn their profession, regretted much seeing Derry quit them; he was a kind, good friend and comrade, and highly honourable in every respect. The morning he set off from Quimper, we escorted him some distance on the road, when we met an Irishman of the name of Mullen, who had just escaped from Ireland, to join the legion; he said that he feared the expedition would have sailed before he arrived. We could learn from him how earnestly the Irish were still looking to France for relief.

Mr. Derry observed to him: "I am quitting the legion and my dear friends here, because I see no chance of an expedition for Ireland." Mr. Mullen was from the county of Down, Mr. Derry's native county, and he had time to get a great deal of news about their common friends, before the coach started, and particularly about his brother, the Catholic bishop, whose diocese was in the county. Mr. Mullen was the nephew of our worthy friend MacCanna, who saved the Irish College in the days of terror.

Mr. Mullen at once had himself enrolled on the books of the Irish legion, determined to stick by it in any rank he could fill. He was not like one of his countrymen, Mr. MacGurken, brother to the Catholic attorney or solicitor, of Belfast, who had been so actively employed in the years 1797 and 1798 defending the United Irishmen then charged with treason. MacGurken thought that the great sacrifices made by his brother at that period entitled him to the rank of officer, and was resolved to accept nothing less. His appearance was greatly against him; he was deeply marked with the smallpox, very ugly in consequence, and along with his disagreeable looks, he was impudent and presumptuous to a degree. He had been a month at Quimper, waiting, as he said, for an answer to an application that had been made in his favour. The non-commissioned officers of the legion were delighted when he went away; they only feared that he might change his mind, and be one day enrolled amongst them.

When Marshal Augereau's corps marched from Brest in 1805, to join the Grand Army, General Arthur O'Connor, who was attached to its staff, came to Paris and married the daughter and only child of the celebrated and unfortunate Condorcet; this union was his great ambition, and indeed it proved a happy one.

Mademoiselle Condorcet had the advantage of being brought up by her high-minded and accomplished mother the Marquise de Condorcet, whose courage and fortitude during the cruel terror and persecution of 1793 acquired for her the greatest consideration from the true patriots of every country; she knew well how to appreciate the sacrifices and sufferings, and imprisonments which Arthur O'Connor had undergone, endeavouring to obtain the freedom of his native country; and her brother, General Grouchy, highly approved of his niece's marriage with his friend General O'Connor.

They were considered a very handsome pair; Mademoiselle Condorcet was a fine, sprightly, animated young girl, scarcely twenty; General O'Connor nearly forty, with very distinguished manners. He soon purchased the estate and *château* de Bignon, in the department of the Loiret, where he spent the greater part of his time, waiting the minister's orders to be actively employed. As nothing was done or attempted by the French Government to better the situation of poor Ireland, during that long war with England, General O'Connor was allowed the full appointments of a general of division, though not in command, till the restoration of the Bourbons, in 1814, when he got a retiring pension of six thousand *francs per annum*.

Several officers of the Irish legion at Quimper, in 1805, were ordered to command detachments to conduct conscripts to Strasbourg: these were Captain Tennant, Captain William Corbet, Lieutenants O'Reilly, Allen, Burgess, O'Morin, etc. At Strasbourg the men were all armed and organised into brigades and columns, to march with all the military preparations and precautions through the country of the Tyrol, to the city of Venice, where the men were drafted into their respective regiments, and the Irish officers got separate "*feuilles de route*" to return by "*étapes*," or regular day's marches, to rejoin the legion at Quimper; besides their pay, they received a marching indemnity, which quite sufficed for them to take the coach occasionally and to visit many places in Italy. This pleasure compensated in a great measure for the painful marches they had to make through the Tyrol mountains. Allen wrote to me frequently during the three months he spent travelling.

In the spring of 1806, during the stay of the legion at Quimper, the English having landed some troops near Concarneau in the night time, Commandant Peterzelli marched with a detachment against them. As he took none of the officers who were Irishmen by birth, and whose turn it was to march, they felt highly indignant at the insult of not being sent against the common enemy; on his return next day, after the English had re-embarked, they went all, without exception, but individually, and deposited their swords with him, declaring they would not resume them till they got satisfaction. They remained eight days for this under forced arrest, when the emperor, hearing of their conduct, and highly approving it, ordered them back their swords, and assured them of his resolution to do them justice.

It was on this occasion we could see that Captain William Lawless possessed great powers of extemporary speaking. He recapitulated in the strongest terms that whether Peterzelli's neglect was intentional or otherwise mattered little; that as officers and men of honour, born in Ireland, we should forthwith seek redress, and surrender our swords till we obtained it. Being under forced arrest, we feared difficulties might occur to prevent our sending off our despatches to the emperor and the Minister of War; but Mrs. Barker soon surmounted them; this excellent woman went, by her husband Captain Barker's orders, and got the document signed by all the Irish officers, and then went three leagues from Quimper and had it put into the post office of a small town on the road to Paris. This precaution was thought advisable.

During the stay of the legion at Quimper, in the spring of 1806, two officers were married there; Captain Masterson to the daughter of the Marquis de Castratt, and Captain Lacy to Mademoiselle Amélie de Guilmar, of a noble family. These marriages created a good deal of amusement, which we needed at the time. Captain Masterson invited several of his comrades to his wedding; and as the Marquis de Castratt had spent some time in the county of Wexford, during his stay in Ireland, at the time of the emigration, we received the kindest hospitality from this elderly nobleman and his daughter, Madame la Comtesse de Beauvoir, a widow lady of great talents and vivacity.

When they had spent the money they brought with them to Ireland, not having the means of getting more from France, Madame de Beauvoir, to support her father, went at once to be governess to the children of Doctor and Mrs. Purcell, of Dublin—parents of the well-known Peter Purcell, who took an active part in the Catholic Association and Precursor society.

Madame de Beauvoir had only been a short time married, when she and her father's family were forced to emigrate; the day they left the *château* to escape to the coast, her husband, the Count de Beauvoir, after going a few hundred yards, returned to the *château* for something he had forgotten; when coming away the second time, he was met by the *gendarmes* in the court, arrested and, shortly after, tried and executed.

The Marquis de Castratt had, besides Madame de Beauvoir, four daughters and a son. Fortunately for those young people, in their father's absence, their uncle, the Marquis de Gregoire, had his daughter married to the first *aide-de-camp* of General Hoche, Colonel Bonté, after the treaty of peace had been concluded with the chiefs of the army of La Vendée. Those chiefs having chosen Mademoiselle de Gregoire to be their *négociatrice* at the headquarters of the French Army, the General-in-Chief Hoche was much taken with her highly accomplished manners, and his *aide-de-camp*, Colonel Bonté, with her person and great beauty. Her name will never be forgotten in Lower Brittany, for the service she rendered, in having the courage to accept this mission in the midst of the cruel civil war then raging there. Colonel Bonté, after his marriage, was soon raised to the rank of general, and got a command in Italy.

Lieutenant O'Reilly, on his way back from Venice, waited on General Bonté, to whose lady he brought a letter from her cousin and former companion, Mademoiselle de Castratt, now Madame Masterson. General Bonté finding O'Reilly speaking French so fluently, told him he would ask the emperor to have him appointed his *aide-de-camp*, with the rank of captain. But O'Reilly could not be persuaded that an expedition would not be sent, sooner or later, to Ireland, therefore he declined the general's friendly offer, which no doubt must afterwards have vexed him, when he was fighting against the English at Flushing, in 1809, still a lieutenant.

Captain Masterson's brother, Mr. John Masterson, who served in the Irish brigades before 1792, and was married to a West India lady, by whom he acquired property in Antigua, was residing at Brussels with his wife and family in 1806. Knowing the Marquis de Castratt in the county of Wexford as a French emigrant, he highly approved his brother's alliance with that nobleman, and settle sixty pounds a year on his sister-in-law, which annuity was paid to her after his death by his daughter, Miss Sally Masterson, who inherited her father's estate in Antigua.

We spent six delightful days with the Marquis de Castratt and his amiable family. In the evenings there was music and dancing on the lawn before the *château* for the country people of the neighbourhood. After supper, little plays were got up, of various kinds, by Madame de Beauvoir and her uncle the Marquis de Gregoire, who had great taste for all such amusements, having learned them when a page to Louis XV; indeed, he possessed much of the polished manners of the old French *noblesse*. What struck us much the day of the wedding, returning from the church through the great hall of the *château*, was to see a number of peasants waiting there to offer presents to the new married pair as they passed. These presents consisted of lambs, kids, calves, rabbits, pigeons, poultry, butter made up in the form of saints, etc.

All being voluntary, the peasantry being no longer serfs, this told well for the Marquis de Castratt. When he returned home from the emigration, he had no power over these peasants, his former tenants or serfs, they had become "proprietors" of the national lands or property. He got back, however, his *château* and gardens, which happened not to have been sold, though plundered and empty. The family had a mansion on the land of their birth, where they were much respected by the country people.

Captain Lacy's marriage with Mademoiselle de Guilmar could not afford us as many amusements, for her uncle, M. de Malesherbes, refused his consent. She had to quit his residence in the country and come to a relation's house at Quimper, who handed her to the altar. When the brave Lacy took her for better, for worse, he never enquired whether she had any fortune or not; she was young, and handsome and sweet-tempered, that was all he required. He gave a splendid supper on the occasion to his comrades and friends. He was born in Spain, and was a real soldier. No Irishman lamented more than he did that the expedition to Ireland did not take place.

A few days after the wedding, we heard that Jerome Buonaparte had returned from America, not accompanied by the ships of the line that sailed from Brest with him, but in a frigate, closely pursued by several English warships. From these he narrowly escaped into the bay of Concarneau, four leagues from Quimper. This little town gave a ball and splendid entertainments to him and the officers of the frigate, whilst he had to wait for orders from the Minister of Marine at Paris. A battalion of infantry was placed on board his frigate to reinforce the crew, lest the English should cut the cable in the night and take her off.

Though we had made no demand collectively to the War Office, yet we heard from our friends at Paris that we might soon expect to change our garrison; and in June, 1806, the legion received orders to march from Quimper to Alençon, there to wait another destination. Before setting out, we heard of poor Lieutenant MacHenry's death at the hospital of Landernau, where he had stopped to be treated for a swelled knee. The surgeon opened it and he died during the operation. He was an honest Presbyterian from the North of Ireland, and a true patriot.

He and I were one day, in March, 1804, taking a walk at Quimper, down the river. Thinking we might meet wolves, we charged our muskets with ball cartridges. Returning, he saw a wild duck dive in the river, and when it put its head up over the water, he fired and killed it; when we examined the duck, we found the ball had split the head in two. So enchanted was he with this musket, that he determined at once to lay out two or three guineas in getting it newly stocked and polished, in the best style. I told him he should try it again before going to any expense, so we went next day to the ruins of an old windmill, a league from the town, and we placed a sheet of paper on the wall. He said he would go about the same distance from the mill that he was from the duck.

After firing three rounds, without once hitting the target, he flung the musket on the ground, swearing at it. He was very good-humoured, and made the officers of the mess laugh at his failure, saying by it he had saved a hundred *francs*. Our march from Quimper could not be agreeable, turning our backs to the coast, and relinquishing, at least for the present, all hopes of Ireland. The married officers were allowed to take the coach as far as Rennes, except Captain Lacy, who was doing the functions of adjutant-major. He had to walk and make the regular day's march.

His lady, on horseback, accompanied him. We had a "*séjour.*" or resting day, at the little town of Pontivy, and another at Rennes, where the legion was reviewed by General Delaborde, who commanded there, and who on this occasion took the privilege to admonish the Irish officers on their too great susceptibility at Quimper with Commandant Peterzelli—who meant nothing, and only, being in great haste to march against the English invaders, took with him the first officers he met belonging to the legion, never thinking of the place of their birth.

This formidable invasion consisted of an English midshipman and ten marine soldiers, who landed in the night and carried off with them two peasants, whom they obliged to dress in their Sunday clothes. These, after sitting all day on board the English frigate as models for the young artists and officers to take their portraits, were landed the night after on the coast, having been well treated during the twenty-four hours of captivity, as prisoners of war should be. These details, though satirical, served to reconcile the officers with Commandant Peterzelli.

General Humbert was residing at Rennes at the time of our passing there, not in favour since his unfortunate failure in Ireland in 1798. Captain Barker, and other officers who knew him at Paris after he returned from prison, waited on him, and found him looking well; he assured them that whenever the French Government was serious about an expedition to Ireland, he would be employed in it.

Admiral Villeneuve, who was taken prisoner at the Battle of Trafalgar, where Nelson fell, in October, 1805, being exchanged and on his way to Paris, stopped at Rennes, and shot himself in the hotel, a few days before the legion arrived there

Our march from Rennes to Alençon was agreeable enough, and as we expected on arriving there to have further orders, we were in great spirits; however, being told that we might hire lodgings, as it was probable that the legion would stop some time, it was thought advisable to send a memorial to the emperor, signed by the officers, praying to be employed on active service; to which the Minister of War answered that his Imperial Majesty would take our demand into consideration. So, we made up our minds to be satisfied with the garrison of Alençon.

I can never forget that it was at this town I received the first letter and news from my dear half-brother, Edward Kennedy, who had suffered three years' imprisonment, and only got liberated under Mr. Fox's administration. He was arrested in August, 1803, a few days after I escaped from Dublin, and the same day, he told me, a general and a minute search was made for me at my mother's residence in the county of Wexford, and at every house in the neighbourhood, where the Orangemen thought I might get shelter.

My brother's letter contained the principal occurrences which took place during his imprisonment, and from the day we separated till his liberation, he never could learn whether or not I had got safe to France, to execute my mission there. Such were the privations the State prisoners had to suffer in the Dublin jails, and no friend was allowed to see them. His melancholy account of poor Robert Emmet's execution made me sad indeed: the body, with the head severed from it, was brought and left for some time in the court of the prison, where the prisoners might view it from their cells.

My brother's greatest comfort was to meet his fellow-prisoners, when they were allowed to walk in the yard, particularly the worthy Philip Long, who proved himself to the last his kind friend: they were liberated the same day; Messrs. Cloney, Hughes, Gray, and Hickson got out some time before.

He spoke to me of William Parrott in the highest terms, which I was very glad of, as his brother Joseph was one of our distinguished officers, and the cousin of my friend and comrade, Hugh Ware; in short, this letter was a complete journal of that sad time: it was brought by some friend of Philip Long's to the Continent, and put into the post office at Amsterdam. I never paid money with such pleasure as I did the four *francs* postage of this letter, which, with my brother's large seal unbroken, and coming to me through an enemy's country, in the time of war, no doubt caused an emotion which can readily be accounted for by the exiles of Erin.

General Bonnet, who commanded the first division of Marshal Augereau's army at Brest, which had been destined for Ireland, was at Alençon on leave of absence when we arrived there. It was said that his dispute with Admiral Ganteaume, about preventing the grenadiers of his division sweeping the decks, did not serve him with the emperor. But he was too brave a soldier, and possessed of too much talent, to be left any time in disgrace by Napoleon, who knew so well how to appreciate the worth of such officers. General Bonnet married a young lady of Alençon whilst we were there.

His brother was the postmaster-general, and enjoyed great influence in the department de l'Orne. Colonel Cavallier, a very handsome man, commanded the *gendarmes* of that country; he and the *préfet* had reception nights, which made the garrison very agreeable. It was at Alençon that the following five officers left the legion in 1806: Captain William Corbet, Captain Bernard MacSheehy, Lieutenant Austin Gibbons, and the Sub-Lieutenants Swanton and Manginean.

CHAPTER 3

Irish Legion Receives Orders for Active Service

We were anxiously following the movements of the French Army in that memorable and short campaign of October, 1806, which decided the fate of the Prussian monarchy at the Battle of Iena on the 14th of the same month; and on the 28th, Napoleon, after he had made his triumphal entrance into the capital of that monarchy, gave orders that the Irish legion should march forthwith to Berlin, there to be completed with men. We now felt that our memorial had succeeded, and we were enchanted at the prospect of seeing real military service. The order for the march sent to the legion at Alençon mentioned the different towns where it was to halt for the night, as far as Mayence. The married officers, as usual, got permission to take the coach with their families, on condition of being present every fifth day at the general inspection.

Captain Barker availed himself of it to place his son Arthur, then nine years of age, in the Irish College at Paris; as the superior required a ministerial order, and it required some days before that could be obtained, the kind Mrs. Tone took charge of little Barker and brought him to her house, to be a playmate for her children, until all the formalities were complied with. I got permission to stop a few days at Paris, to see some of my friends who were still there: Mr. John Sweetman, Lewins, MacCormack, etc.

By taking the coach to Château-Thierry, I rejoined the legion there at the inspection. Although we did not muster very strong, still we were organised as completely as the French regiments; each company having its captain, lieutenant, sub-lieutenant, sergeant-major, sergeants, corporals and drummers; and, besides the eagle-bearer, who had the rank of officer, the ensign-bearer with the green colours, on which was "The Independence of Ireland "inscribed in gold letters. And on the other side of the green colours was the "Harp without the Crown."

With our eagle uncovered and colours flying, we marched in perfect military order through every town, and excited great interest amongst the inhabitants, who used to exclaim, that, the Irish and the Poles were their faithful allies. The town of Verdun, where we should have halted one night, being the depot of the English prisoners of war, the governor took upon himself to lodge the Irish legion in a suburb, lest its presence might be disagreeable to those prisoners; at daybreak he had the drawbridge let down and the gates opened to let the legion march through, before the English prisoners could have light to see and contemplate our green flag, and its beautiful inscription, so obnoxious to them, "The Independence of Ireland!"

Our march, however, through the town at that early hour attracted great notice; as our band played up our national air of "Patrick's Day in the Morning," we could see many windows opened, and gentlemen in their shirts enquiring across the street, in good English, what was meant by this music at such an early hour. "Why, damn it, Burke, you ought to know that air," was answered from one window to another. This caused much conversation.

Although we were not very well lodged in the faubourg of Verdun, we had a capital dinner in one of the little inns there. I sat at table next to Captain O'Heren, who entertained us with many anecdotes of what occurred in 1792, when the place was garrisoned by the Prussian army.

At four leagues from Verdun, on the road to Metz, we halted in a village to breakfast, and it was amusing enough to hear all the news that the officers had learned at their lodgings, the night before, respecting the English prisoners, and their rambles through the country, every day till sunset, when they had to be in town to answer the roll call.

Captain O'Heren got permission at the village to take the coach as far as Metz, and we were greatly shocked on arriving there next day to learn that he had died suddenly in the night at the hotel where he stopped. O'Heren was studying in France at the time of the Revolution, and took an active part in it: he had talent, and would have filled a diplomatic situation with credit. He and I were lodged in the same house at Lesneven, where he was a great favourite with the family, who received a good deal of company in the evening. O'Heren's society they considered a great acquisition; he spoke French fluently, and had the gay manners of a well-bred Irishman; he was a good patriot, and could not fail to be well received wherever he went.

Our march continued to be agreeable enough, the weather being very fine, though at the end of November. Arriving at Sarrebruck, we halted to breakfast there. The town had been burnt, and suffered much from the disasters of the war. It was in this place that Pitt had established a manufactory of forged assignats, as one of his famous stratagems for ruining and conquering the French nation!

On arriving at Mayence, the legion received orders to halt there, where 1,500 Poles who had been in the Prussian service volunteered to enter into the French service after the Battle of Iena. They were incorporated into the Irish legion at Mayence, as were a great number of Irish. These Irish had been engaged in the rebellion, and whilst imprisoned in Ireland were sold by the English Government, in 1798 and 1799, to the King of Prussia, to work in his mines; his agent going through the prisons in Ireland and choosing the best and ablest young men. Previous to the hostilities with France, the King of Prussia obliged these brave and unfortunate men to enter his army. It may easily be imagined they rejoiced to join the Irish soldiery in the service of France; holding out a hope, as it then did, that they would one day see their country liberated.

Those Irish Prussian prisoners, speaking German, so as to make themselves understood, and at least as well as their comrades the Polish prisoners, rendered vast service to their officers in the beginning. We met amongst them many whom we knew in the insurrection of 1798; Captain Ware met several who had fought beside him in the county of Kildare, *viz*.: Foster, Gunning, etc., fine young fellows. And Dalton, Cane, Doyle, O'Brien, and many others, were from the counties of Wexford and Wicklow, who knew me from my childhood. Malony, who had been wounded at Castlebar, and condemned to be transported, had the rank of sergeant-major in the Prussian Army; he soon obtained that of officer of the Irish legion, and became one of the distinguished captains of the Irish regiment in the campaigns of 1813.

The French pay, the soldiers' rations, and the way of living, with the discipline, was so much superior to that of the Prussian Army, that both Poles and Irish were delighted with the French service. Marshal Kellerman, who commanded the army of reserve at Mayence, gave orders that great coats, shirts, shoes, etc., should be furnished forthwith to the captains of the Irish legion for their soldiers, and in a few days after, on passing the review, he was quite pleased to see the legion so well equipped and so formidable.

He paid us some handsome compliments on this occasion, saying, that the Irish bravery was proverbial, and their attachment to France well known, etc. He also told us that he had been a cadet in one of the Irish brigades when a boy, for a short time. His manners were simple, and those of a well-bred gentleman; his military career long and glorious; but he prided himself more on his victory at Valmy than on all the others, because he said, it put an end for ever to the Prussian ambition of making conquests in France.

We found Mayence a delightful garrison, though on account of the continual passage of troops there, and its being the great depot of the Grand Army, we could not expect to remain longer than the time necessary to get our men armed. We used to meet, on the public walk, the Empress Josephine and her daughter Hortense, Queen of Holland, both looking young and handsome.

At a concert given to them, the son of our master tailor, young Flechy, a lad of fourteen years of age, played on the violin, to the surprise and admiration of the other musicians, who considered him quite a prodigy. The empress, next day, sent him a handsome present.

At the end of December, the legion was ordered to march to Landau; this town being a strong fortress where the service of the place was executed with as much punctuality and rigor as if the enemy were at its gates, was of the greatest service to both officers and men.

On this march to Landau, Captain Ware and I got permission to cross the Rhine and visit the town of Manheim, of which there has been so much said of its beauty and regularity. Having to recross the river early next morning, to join our companies that were lodged in a village on the road, we were not a little surprised to hear volleys of musket-shots in every direction; on enquiring, we were told that it was the custom of the country to celebrate the new year with this kind of rejoicing at daybreak: so our march to Landau, on the first of January, 1807, accompanied by rejoicing and firing, announced that we should see, ere the war terminated, plenty of that kind of amusement.

The Irish legion was well received by the inhabitants of Landau; they recollected the noble conduct of Captain Harty in 1792, when he, in spite of his Lieutenant-Colonel, O'Mahony, prevented Berwick's regiment from crossing the Rhine to the enemy's camp, and marched back with it in triumph. He received the grateful thanks of the governor, and of the people of the town. Is not this circumstance one of the instances which show how difficult it is to define what is called passive obedience to military chiefs and tyrants? Had Captain Harty obeyed his chief, the French Army would have been deprived of the splendid services of the 70th Demi-Brigade, and the Irish composing it would have been driven to the cruel and dishonourable necessity of soliciting employment from the British Government!

No garrison could be more suitable for the completion of the legion than Landau; provisions there were cheap and abundant, particularly potatoes, which the Polish soldiers relished fully as much as the Irish did. Their manner of preparing this food was excellent. The potatoes were grated, then half boiled into a sort of soup; a quantity of bacon being cut very small and half fried, was put into the potato soup, and boiled until it became quite thick, then it was turned out into the soldiers' dishes or pans. They enjoyed this pudding very much, though it did not contain any currants or raisins. With such substantial diet, our soldiers were able to bear up against fatigue and the cold frosty weather, and accordingly we had exercise and manoeuvring every day, though in the depth of winter.

Hearing that there were Prussian prisoners arrived at the town of Spires, and that one of them, a man seven feet high, wished to engage in a French regiment as "drum-major," I was sent there, and my instructions were, not to engage any of them but Poles, except, however, the *tambour*-major (drum-major), whose birthplace mattered not, provided he could march upright at the head of the legion. The commander of the town of Spires gave me the best assistance he could; I dined with him, and after dinner he sent for the giant, as he called him, and asked him what was the amount of the Prussian pay he received.

We found that the French pay would be double; besides, the officers consented to add forty *francs* a month to it; so, with all this, and the double rations he was entitled to, the *tambour*-major was enchanted, and he told me he would be ready to march when I pleased. He had got a slight wound, but the surgeon of the hospital who visited him assured me that it would never prevent him from marching and doing his service. Forty of the Poles volunteered; only thirty of them were fit for marching; I engaged these, gave each a day's pay, and ordered them to assemble at eight o'clock next morning, when we started for Landau, and after marching more than three leagues, I halted in a village for an hour to let the men breakfast, and when the drum beat to march again, all were present, but the frost was so intense, twelve degrees under zero, that half of the men were seized with the cold and unable to proceed, in consequence of having quitted the red-hot stoves in the houses where they had breakfasted.

By the time I arrived at the gates of Landau, in the evening, only ten of the thirty were present; the other twenty being so weak, they took two days to come to Landau. The chief and all the officers were delighted to see the *superbe tambour*-major and paid me many compliments for the care I had taken of him on the march, keeping him away from the hot stoves, and only allowing him to drink what was necessary to bear up against the desperate cold, otherwise he also would have remained sick on the road. The inhabitants admired the *tambour*-major, as they did everything that added splendour to the troops of the garrison, on whom depended a good deal of the commerce of Landau, furnishing the ornaments, and everything in the way of provisions.

The apartments let to the officers insured a small rent to the housekeepers, who were attentive and careful to make everything comfortable in the lodgings. It was edifying to witness the tolerance amongst these good people with regard to religion. In the same church, every Sunday, the Catholics and the Protestants had, at different hours, their respective religious services. We went to the nine o'clock Mass, and, leaving the church, we used to meet at the door the Protestants entering for their worship, which began at ten. This was an agreeable sight to us who were brought up with a horror of the Protestant ascendancy in Ireland.

We spent the gay time of carnival at Landau, and were very happy there; but we were rejoiced when the order arrived for the legion to march to the camp at Boulogne-sur-Mer, as this march to the coast indicated that Napoleon had not relinquished his former great plan of invading England and Ireland, and that he would resume it on a larger scale, when he concluded peace with Russia and Prussia.

The camp at Boulogne was then commanded by one of the illustrious captains of the age, the Colonel-General Gouvion Saint-Cyr, afterwards a marshal of France. The army of reserve under his orders was principally composed of the fourth or fifth battalions of the regiments of the Grand Army, which left their depots at the different camps on the coast to receive the young soldiers, and there to have them instructed and prepared for campaigning. To make part of an army commanded by one of the ablest generals of the time, delighted us, and we were gay and cheerful on the way.

At Metz we had a resting day, where the council of administration ordered two thousand feathers and other ornaments to be made, and forwarded to the camp at Boulogne. On this march the legion was not lodged in the suburbs of Verdun; But the English prisoners there could behold, from the ramparts, at half a league off, a little army on march, clothed in green, commanded by Irish officers, with the eagle uncovered, and the banners flying, on which was inscribed, in large letters of gold, "Independence of Ireland."

At Arras, though there was a depot of English prisoners there, we were lodged in the town, because the governor had the good sense to make the English sleep one night in the citadel, until we marched out in the morning.

We found everything in perfect order on arriving at our camp at Boulogne-sur-Mer: the soldiers' barracks, as well as those of the officers, were clean and airy. A few hours sufficed for us to be completely installed in our new abode; the inhabitants at Boulogne being so well accustomed to furnish every necessary for the military, we had no trouble, and for the sum of twelve *francs* a month, an officer's barrack was furnished with bed, table, chairs, etc.

On the third day after our arrival, we were reviewed by the general-in-chief, Gouvion Saint-Cyr; it was the first time I had seen him. And now transcribing these notes, I am reminded of a short conversation he honoured me with in 1819, when he was Minister of War to Louis XVIII.

The Inspector-General Claperode had the half-pay officers of the department of the Seine assembled at his house in the Rue Ville-l'Evêque, when he conducted them across the Place de la Concorde to the Minister of War's hotel in the Rue Saint-Dominique to pay their respects to His Excellency; the officers, in the different uniforms of the empire, formed a motley group, and caused a sensation; mine, being green, attracted notice as well as the others. The minister asked me if I had obtained my letters of naturalisation. I said to him I had. Then other questions about my campaigns.

He then wished to know if I possessed any fortune: "None but my sword, *monsieur le maréchal*," was my reply; on which he bowed to me. Twelve days after, I received my commission for the 2nd battalion of the Second Legion de l'Ille-et-Vilaine, then forming at Rennes. Unfortunately, before the 2nd battalion had time to be assembled, a re-organisation of the French Army into regiments took place, by which change I had still to remain on half pay.

To return to Boulogne, our men being mostly soldiers who had served, it only required some drilling and exercise to make them understand the French word of command, to enable us to manoeuvre in line with the French regiments. One month busily and well employed at the camp of Boulogne sufficed to accomplish this: and at a grand review passed there by the general-in-chief, Gouvion Saint-Cyr, he testified his satisfaction on the progress which the Irish legion had made in manoeuvring; and the brilliancy of its *tenue* pleased him much; indeed, it appeared to great advantage at the review, having got in time from Metz the feathers and the other ornaments for the soldiers; altogether their uniform was splendid.

A very disagreeable circumstance occurred this day; the following is a true version of it. A vain Prussian captain, of the name of Delorme, in whom Marshal Kellerman had taken some interest at Mayence, was attached to the legion and followed it to the camp at Boulogne-sur-Mer.

At a general review passed by General Saint-Cyr, when the legion, in column by companies, was marching to defile before the general-in-chief, Captain Delorme, who had no company in the legion, wishing to show himself by defiling before the general, and perceiving Lieutenant Powell commanding a company in the absence of his captain, who was sick, insisted on taking the command from the lieutenant, who refused, stating he saw no order from the chief to give up the command of his company at that time, and having passed the review and inspection all day, he wished to have the honour of defiling before the general; but the captain persevering, the lieutenant pushed him rudely from before the company, and continued to defile.

As soon as the review was over, Captain Delorme complained to Commandant Peterzelli, who had Lieutenant Powell sent to the town prison, where he was to remain till he was tried by a court-martial. Upon this, all the other lieutenants of the legion resolved to force Captain Delorme to fight them, and drew lots. Lieutenant Allen, who spoke to him first on the subject, and whom he refused to fight, was immediately sent to the town prison. Lieutenant O'Reilly meeting Delorme in the fields, coming from the chief's lodgings, after having had Lieutenant Allen sent to prison, told him he must fight on the spot, or give him his word of honour that he would fight as soon as he could procure a second. He complied with the latter demand, and went to Boulogne to get a captain of a Swiss regiment to be his second. They fought with swords, and Lieutenant O'Reilly might have easily killed or wounded him, as he asked several times to repose himself, and finally said he would fight no more.

Lieutenant Powell was tried by the court-martial at the camp at

Ambleteuse. The court was presided by General Dufour, who had been in the expedition to Ireland, and who felt for the persecuted Irish. Mr. MacCanna, a worthy Irish patriot established at Boulogne, got a worthy friend of his, a major in one of the regiments, to defend Lieutenant Powell, and never was a defence more ably conducted. The comparison between the Irish and the Prussians, and the devotion of the former to the French cause, was so forcibly stated, that it appeared a shame to have let the trial take place. Lieut. Powell was accordingly acquitted with great *éclat*.

Lieutenant Allen, on coming out of prison, sent a challenge by Captain Dowdall to Captain Delorme, who, however, preferred signing a paper, saying, that if he could not obtain an exchange into some other regiment in the course of six months, he would give in his resignation. After this, he lived on good terms with the officers.

During the stay of the legion at the camp, the six following officers were ordered to Brest, where still hopes were held out of an expedition to Ireland: Captains Lawless, Markey, and Brangan, and Lieutenants Murray, O'Reilly, and Devereux.

In June, 1807, the legion was ordered to march from Boulogne to Antwerp. This town being declared in a state of siege, the garrison duty was severe, and strictly executed, much to the advantage of the young officers. General Harty had the command of the brigade, of which the legion made a part. The senator Lefebvre was the governor-general of Antwerp.

Many ships of the line were launched at this time at Antwerp.

Charles Ryan, who came from Dublin, joined the legion at Antwerp, but not being personally known to any of the officers, and having no papers with him to prove his identity, he found some difficulty on arriving, especially as the governor had no instructions from the Minister of War respecting him. Captain Ware knowing his father in Dublin, volunteered to be responsible for him, and he was accordingly allowed to follow the legion till he received his commission as sub-lieutenant from the Minister of War in July, 1808.

Putting Antwerp in a state of siege was necessary, no doubt, and where there were such vast naval stores, the military service required to be rigorously executed, in order to be always guarded against an enemy so powerful at sea as the English were at that period. Napoleon's great victories, and the peace he concluded at Tilsit in July, 1807, with the Prussian and Russian monarchs, did not save the poor King of Denmark, who was in profound peace with all the world, from having his capital, Copenhagen, bombarded; his fleet, consisting of twenty-eight sail of the line, sixteen frigates, nine brigs, and a number of small vessels being seized, and all his naval and military stores being taken or destroyed, a month after that peace of Tilsit, by the English robbers, who felt no shame at so foul a deed.

At Antwerp, four officers of the Irish legion mounted guard every day, besides those making the rounds at night. My post was generally at the arsenal every eight or ten days, where I did not find the twenty-four hours of guard dull, having so much to see and admire in the construction of those ships of the line, so rapidly completed, three being launched whilst we were in garrison at Antwerp—the *Austerlitz*, *Iena*, and *Friedland*.

General Chamberlac, who commanded the military division at Brussels, was appointed to inspect the troops comprising the garrison and forts of Antwerp. His inspection lasted eight days, during which time we were busily occupied with the theory, exercise and evolutions. His report on the state of the instruction and discipline of the Irish legion was very favourable, and highly flattering to the officers; so much so, that the brave General Harty, who commanded our brigade, promised us, that he would have no manoeuvres for some time, in order that we might have a little recreation after our fatigues.

We eagerly availed ourselves of his politeness, and organised country excursions to offer amusements to the married officers' ladies of the regiment Captain Masterson's niece, Miss Sally Masterson, was on a visit with him and his wife at the time, and she being very handsome, highly educated, sprightly and amiable in her manners, attracted much attention. She soon became the delight of all who knew her.

Captain Dowdall and other officers decided on spending a day at the fort of Lillo, four leagues down the river, and they hired a large sloop to bring the guests, with the band of the legion, wines, and everything necessary for a splendid dinner, to which the governor of the fort was invited, along with the mayor of the village of Lillo. The weather was bright and warm, and the table was laid out in a shady garden belonging to the hotel. After seeing all that was curious in the fort, we sat down to dinner.

The ladies being placed at table between the French gentlemen, gave great assistance in doing the honours. The conversation turning on the beautiful effect of the music, as we sailed into Lillo, Captain Ware asked Captain Dowdall "if Commandant Peterzelli appeared displeased at not being invited to be of the party, when he called on him to ask permission to bring the band of the regiment on board?"

Poor Dowdall exclaimed, "I entirely forgot to get it, I had so many other things to think of." On which there was a general laugh, and he blushed still more deeply, when someone said: "A man in love cannot have all his wits about him!"

The fact was, Dowdall took charge of all, and he even had the precaution to bring several of our soldiers who were first rate seamen also, to aid the sailors of the vessel; unfortunately, he forgot the precaution of limiting the quantity they were to drink, so that, although Regan, Gallagher, Harrison, etc., were well-behaved, sober soldiers, they were this day, like the rest of the company, half seas over on leaving Lillo, and could neither steer nor row a boat to tow on our sloop; so that, before we had got half way up the river to Antwerp, some of the ladies became alarmed, and screamed out begging to be put on shore. It being also the wish of Father Cowan, who had charge of Miss Sally Masterson, we had the vessel brought as near to the banks as possible, when almost all the company landed.

Captain and Mrs. Barker, Captain Ware, and a few others, preferred remaining on board all night. But, luckily for them, the wind changed, and they reached Antwerp before the gates were shut; whilst all of us who had landed, passed a wretched enough night in a farmhouse half a league from the river, and early in the morning made the best of our way to Antwerp on foot; we, however, procured a large waggon for the ladies before we started.

We officers, not having had permission to be absent for a night from a town in a state of siege, were put under arrest for four days, when we arrived at Antwerp. Miss Sally Masterson hearing this, went at once to General Harty, and brought him with her to the governor, whom she prayed to raise our arrests, declaring that she was the cause of our not returning before night to Antwerp, as she had become so alarmed in the ship. Of course, the governor could not refuse the petition of so fair a lady, and so our arrests were immediately raised.

Miss Sally Masterson did not return home till she had the pleasure herself of visiting and announcing to the various officers her success with the governor. She said to the governor, when asking him to raise our arrests, that she was emboldened to do so, from being the daughter of an officer who had served in France, and the niece of a Captain of the Irish legion, and particularly as she had been the cause of the vessel being delayed in sailing up the river, for, from her delicate health, she was easily alarmed, etc. Indeed, Miss Masterson did look very delicate, and the more so from being in deep mourning for her father, who had died a short time before at Brussels. Her mother and her younger sister came to join her at Antwerp, where they took an "*appartement*" on the Place Verte, and where they gave very agreeable evening tea parties.

We met there sometimes Mrs. Masterson of Bruges, and her two daughters, Miss Mary and Miss Martha. In marching through Bruges, I had the pleasure of dining with them, on our way to Antwerp, and they introduced us to a very worthy Scotch gentleman, a friend of theirs, a Mr. Johnstone, who was the Austrian consul at Antwerp. Mrs. Masterson and her two daughters were at this time on a visit to Mr. and Mrs. Johnstone. They were English, and no relation to the other Masterson family. Miss Martha Masterson little thought then that, two years later, she would have it in her power to succour and save the life of an Irish exile.

In 1808 she married an eminent physician at Flushing, a Dr. Moke, and on the 15th of August while the French general, Monet, was negotiating to obtain good terms from Lord Chatham, but before the capitulation was signed, Commandant William Lawless was brought desperately wounded to Madame Moke's house. She had him immediately carefully placed in her cellar on a mattrass, when she gave him refreshments herself, until her husband returned at night, and had time to examine and dress his wound. Nothing could exceed their kind attention to Lawless, and to Lieutenant O'Reilly, his fellow sufferer, until they procured them the means of escaping from the isle of Walcheren to Antwerp, nearly three months after. (These men were liable to be hanged as rebels by the English if captured. S. G.)

When Miss Sally Masterson and her mother and sister were going to return to Brussels, we agreed to conduct them as far as Malines, which is half-way, and there to have a farewell dinner. Mrs. and Miss Masterson of Bruges were going at the same time to spend some time at Brussels, so we had the pleasure of their company also at the parting dinner at Malines. Captain Dowdall had an elegant *char-à-banc* of his own, with a very fine horse; this carriage was quite adapted for little country parties in fine weather; it had three seats which held three persons each, and one on the coach box drove.

This time Mr. Allen drove the *char-à-banc*. Nothing could be more agreeable than our dinner party at Malines, till the doleful moment of parting arrived; then Dowdall, on taking leave, made a great harangue or speech, which he concluded by saying, "May God forget us, if we ever forget you!" This, of course, was addressed to Miss Sally.

After seeing the two families of Masterson into their carriages, and set off for Brussels, Captains Dowdall and Allen, with seven or eight ladies (of the Irish legion), got up into the *char-à-banc*. Allen volunteered again to drive, got up on the box, and fearing that the gates of Antwerp might be shut before they could get there, they drove off at a prodigiously rapid rate. Lieutenant Gillmor and I had a carriage for ourselves, and he having taken the precaution to get a permission in the morning before leaving town, to have the gates opened for us till 12 o'clock, we were in no hurry, and were the last on the road.

After making three leagues, we perceived three of our party, who had been thrown from the *char-à-banc* on the highway; Captain Masterson's wife was endeavouring to carry one of the wheels another lady something else. The horse had escaped into a field, and Allen and Dowdall were in pursuit of him. As to the *char-à-banc*, it was smashed in pieces, and they were only trying to save the horse. No one was hurt, and Gillmor and I hastened to stow all the ladies into our carriage, and followed them close on foot to have the gates opened.

After conducting them to their houses, we repaired to our homes; we were very wet, as it had rained the whole way. This party concluded the *fêtes* got up for Miss Sally Masterson while she was on the visit to her uncle and aunt. However, on hearing of our misadventures, and fearing that some of her friends might have been injured when the *char-à-banc* broke down, she came back to Antwerp to ascertain the particulars. She was accompanied this time by a Miss Stanhope, a friend of hers, a very handsome young lady, whose family resided at Brussels. After visiting all her friends, Miss Sally Masterson returned the next day to Brussels; it was the last time that any of us had the pleasure of seeing her.

Although in time of war, many found means of getting away from Ireland and came to France through Holland, or by Hamburgh. Mr. Putnam MacCabe, whom we left at Paris in 1803, when we were hurrying off to the coast to embark, as we thought, in an expedition to liberate our country from a foreign yoke, arrived one morning at Antwerp, in the month of August, 1807, from Amsterdam. He was accompanied by two ladies whom he had taken charge of in London, Mrs. Berthemy and her daughter; they were the sister and the niece of the celebrated Irish orator, Henry Flood, the contemporary of Grattan. MacCabe being well known to many of the officers, we invited him and the two ladies, his fellow travellers, to dine at our mess at the

Lion-d'Or; they accepted our invitation, and we spent a very pleasant evening. MacCabe showed us a beautiful case of duelling pistols, which he was taking to offer as a present to his friend General Arthur O'Connor, then at Paris.

A few days after, an officer of the former Irish brigade, Captain Wall, arrived at Antwerp, with his wife, two sons and three daughters; they had passed the time of the emigration at Wexford, where he carried on some kind of business in the salt trade. Arriving at Paris, he got his sons into the Irish College to finish their studies, and he himself got placed as a captain at the depot of the Irish legion. His wife was a Miss Walsh, born in France, and cousin to the Count de Leran Walsh, senator.

In September, 1807, the Irish legion was ordered to the isle of Walcheren, and encamped at West Capelle, two leagues from Flushing. The legion at this time was considerably augmented by Polish and Irish recruits arriving daily; but it suffered dreadfully from the effects of the climate, General Harty, who commanded the brigade, with half the officers and men, being sick at one time. In consequence of which, the camp was raised and the legion was ordered to Ter Verre and Middleburg, in November, as being more healthy quarters; the hospitals in those towns were soon crowded with officers as well as men.

A battalion of eight hundred men being ordered to Spain, Captain Lacy got the command, being the senior officer of those who were not sick. This battalion made part of the army that went into Spain with Prince Murat. They followed him to Madrid, and encamped in its vicinity in the winter of 1807 and 1808, remaining there till the revolt of May 2, 1808, when it was ordered into Madrid to make part of the garrison of that capital. From thence it retreated back behind the Ebro with King Joseph in the summer of 1808, and, being continually employed at the advanced posts, suffered much.

Before the battalion received orders to march from Madrid, Captain Lacy disappeared. Being a Spaniard by birth, he had numerous acquaintances in Madrid, and it was thought at first that he had fallen a victim to some jealous rival, particularly as his horse, money and effects of every kind were found at his lodgings, and his servant could give no clue where he might be found.

It was only at the Battle of Ocano, the year after, that it was rightly known what had become of him: there he commanded a brigade of Spanish cavalry against the French, and escaped amongst the last from the field of battle. He was afterwards named Captain-General of Catalonia by the Cortes of Cadiz, and was one of their devoted sup-

MADRID UPRISING, 1808

porters; but after the return of King Ferdinand from imprisonment in France, Lacy, being considered too liberal, soon fell into disgrace with His Majesty, who suspected him to be at the head of a conspiracy in favour of the Constitution of 1812. He was tried by a court-martial, condemned to death, and sent to the island of Majorca, where his guards shot him as soon as he landed

The remainder of the Irish legion that was left in Holland returned from Ter Verre and Middleburg to Flushing in December, 1807, to be under the orders of General Monet, governor-general of the isle of Walcheren.

Flushing was at this time, by a decree of the emperor, separated from Holland and annexed to France. It was inundated in 1808, from the dykes giving way in a great storm, when numbers lost their lives. The Irish officers received great praise for their active exertions on this melancholy occasion, by which many lives were saved; and, as on all such, where the lives of human beings were in danger, Allen was one of those officers sure to be found ready to risk his own life to save that of others. He and I were lodged at a hotel on the most elevated part of Flushing. The evening before this disastrous inundation took place, we went to call on Captain Barker and his wife; they had just arrived from Middleburg, and were lodged on a ground floor of a private house, by billet. They promised to come and breakfast with us early the next morning, and we were to assist them in looking out for comfortable lodgings.

In the morning, Allen remained at our hotel to see that the breakfast was properly prepared, whilst I went to conduct the Barkers to our hotel, as they did not know the town. I had hardly gone fifty steps from the hall-door, when I saw the sea rolling mountains high, and the quays covered with eight feet of water. The floods had risen, and were more than fifteen feet deep in the street, where the Barkers were lodged. Boats were getting ready, and Allen and I hired one, and pointed to the sailors to row to the street where Captain Barker was lodged. Seeing that the water had reached the first storey of his house, where Captains Ware and Parrot were both lying sick in bed of the Flushing fever, we, of course, thought they were drowned.

However, on sailing under the windows of the house, we saw Captain Barker at one of them on the third floor; he told us their escape was a mere chance, and owing to their little child, Alice, sleeping in a cradle bed beside them. She was awoke by the water flowing upon her, and called out loudly, "Mamma, mamma, salt water, salt water!"

They had just time to rush to the stairs, carrying the child. One minute more, and it would have been too late, as the sea soon invaded the first storey, where Ware and his cousin were. They had time to get out of bed, carry up their clothes and get to the garret to dress themselves.

We soon brought them a small basket of provisions, enough for the day, and which they pulled up by a rope. We then went to one of the lowest streets of the town, where the magazine of the legion was stowed. There we found the front of the house thrown down by the flood, and the master tailor, Flecher, and several men holding by the rafters of the third storey. We procured a ladder, and got them safe into our boat. But all the cloth and arms, and everything in the house, was carried away into the sea, by the flood and returning tide. Allen and I continued going from street to street enquiring about the officers who were blockaded by the inundation.

Arthur MacMahon's account of the way his landlady and her family perished was lamentable indeed. He lodged on the first floor, and the family under him on the ground one. The unfortunate woman's cries awakened him, and he ran downstairs to try to get her out of the water, when he himself narrowly escaped being drowned. A mountain of water flowed in, and the cries ceased! Never, to his last moments, could MacMahon forget these cries.

I had, unfortunately, to quit Allen suddenly, and repair to bed, there to pass five or six hours in cold and hot fits, knocked down with a terrible fever, whilst he remained at the great guard-house all night, giving orders, or going with relief to the unfortunate inhabitants, many of whom were saved by his timely exertions at that perilous moment; a report of which was published next day, and a complimentary letter, signed by the civil authorities of Flushing, was addressed to him. I must add, he prized this letter as equal to any brevet he ever obtained afterwards in campaign.

In all kind of danger, even in sickness, Allen was lucky. I recollect when he, Ware, Parrot, Eager, Gillmor, O'Reilly and I were in the officer's ward in the military hospital at Middleburg, that he got rid of his fever in eight days, and had scarcely ever any relapse; whereas we had it returning continually until we left the island.

Although the inhabitants of Flushing at the time of the disastrous inundation were no longer the subjects of the King of Holland, Louis Buonaparte, yet his human compassion was no way wanting towards them in their misfortunes. He sent large sums of money to be distributed amongst the people who had lost their all. Few monarchs at that period, 1808, could boast of being so beloved as he was by his Dutch subjects.

This fearful inundation took place in the month of January, 1808.

The French troops in garrison at Flushing always received the same pay and rations as the Dutch Army; and this was equal to double that of the French pay, until the annexation of the town to the French Empire took place, when they were paid only according to the French tariff, which was a great privation in that bad climate, and where everything was so dear. The soldiers, however, continued to receive rations of wine.

Captain Ware never could have recovered, had he remained at Flushing, he was so reduced by the fever; but, fortunately for him, he got an order to join the battalion of the legion then encamped at Madrid, with Prince Murat, a captain's place being vacant in it.

Our surgeon-major, Saint-Leger, being in a dying state, I had to call on Dr. Moke, one of the first physicians in Flushing. Seeing the worst symptoms, my feet greatly swelled, and that the great quantity of bark that I had taken did not stop the fever, he advised me of all things to get a change of air. Having obtained in consequence of his certificate a leave of absence for a month, I took my passage in a vessel going up to Antwerp, and engaged two of the sailors to come to my hotel, to help me to get on board in time, as the vessel sailed at break of day. We reached Antwerp that same evening, time enough for me to take the coach for Brussels.

I stopped at the Hotel de Flandre in that town, and next day had a visit of a worthy Irish patriot, Mr. Corr, who had been established a considerable time in business in Brussels; he told me that, hearing that one of the officers of the Irish legion in garrison at Flushing had arrived sick at the hotel, he called to offer his services, and to see if there was anything he could do for him. He wished to know if I found the hotel to my liking; I answered that it was everything I could desire, and the charges very reasonable; the only thing I could object to was, the dinner hour, half-past one o'clock, which was too soon for me.

On this he said, that he and Mrs. Corr dined always at half-past four, or five o'clock at the latest, and that he was sure the hour and their dinner would suit my taste, and that I could pay them the same price I was to give at the Hotel de Flandre. Not knowing Mr. Corr's circumstances, and thinking that it might be of use to him, I consented, and, the same day, I began to dine with him and his amiable wife. He hired a lodging for me two doors from his own house, with very obliging people, who prepared my breakfast for me, quite to my mind; so I was most comfortably settled. Every day I felt improving, and the fever nearly subsided It being carnival time, Brussels, as usual, kept up its renown for all kinds of merriment during that period; there were plays, masked balls, etc. I think these amusements, with the good fare I had at Mr. Corr's, roused me after the irksome, desponding life I had led at Middleburg and Flushing.

The former place is a most beautiful town: its cleanliness and neatness beyond all description, but to spend a Sunday there would suffice to throw one into the lowest spirits. Such are the religious habits of the Puritans who inhabit that pretty town, that they scruple even to open their doors on a Sunday to give directions to a stranger how to find his way. I have experienced this inconvenience; meeting no one in the street, I had to ring at two or three houses before anyone would condescend to open the door and speak to me, yet at every house there were people at the windows.

To add to my comfort during the three weeks and four days which I was allowed to remain at Brussels, the worthy Father Cowan, whom I had had the pleasure of knowing at Antwerp the year before, was there; he used to call on me to take me out to walk with him in the park, and as he belonged to the cathedral, he knew the town well. We used to stop at a cake shop, eat some cakes and take a glass of good sherry wine before separating. I told him on what conditions I had accepted Mr. Corr's table. He laughed and said:

> I see you don't know Corr; but don't mind him, there is a way of being up to him. His hospitality is well known to his countrymen; as to his wife, she is a woman of the greatest merit, and a lady in every sense of the word; they are both much respected, and deservedly so.

Father Cowan used to dine occasionally on Sundays at Mr. Corr's, and he was most agreeable and full of amusing anecdotes. He had travelled much and studied and passed many years at Prague; he spoke German, Italian, and French as well as English. No "Pat" ever regretted more than he did not to be able to speak his native tongue, Irish.

My leave of absence being expired, I had to quit in haste and take leave of my good friends, whom I can never forget; for it to was their kind attention in a great measure that I owed my recovery at Brussels in so short a time. I had to stop a day at Antwerp for a vessel going to Flushing, and next evening I rejoined my comrades in that town. I need not say they were agreeably surprised to see me so well recovered.

I returned very *apropos*, as one of the emperor's *aides-de-camp*, General Bertrand, came shortly after to inspect the troops of the garrison, and to give instructions to General Monet, governor of the island, respecting the fortifications, defence to be made, etc., etc. We had, for several days, reviews, inspections, and manoeuvres, and as I belonged to the grenadiers' company, it was lucky for me that I had got rid of my fever, at least for some time; and I resolved for the future to remain at my post, at all hazards, until an order to send troops to reinforce the battalion in Spain should arrive, and not to be absent, either at the hospital, or on leave of absence. The year before, had I only been sick in my room, instead of being at the hospital, I should have marched with the battalion commanded by Captain Lacy to Madrid.

At Flushing an excellent *table-d'hôte* was kept by an Englishman of the name of Holder, where several of our officers dined at five o'clock. I went to dine there for some time; we had very agreeable company. General Clement lodged in the hotel, and his *aides-de-camp* dined with us, and occasionally the naval officers of the men-of-war ships lying in the roads. From the too frequent night service, making rounds in the damp air and fogs, I felt I should have a relapse of the horrid fever and ague. I had to quit the good table and begin again to take the Jesuit's bark, the only remedy Dr. Moke could prescribe. He was good enough to give me some he had in reserve for himself of a superior quality, and which could not be had at the chemist's; taking this red bark with strong port wine, I used to keep off the fever for a few days.

The newly-appointed French captain of the port of Flushing lodged in the same hotel with me, and as the smugglers were sure to bring English newspapers, he had orders to send them forthwith to Paris. He frequently asked me to look over these newspapers, as he did not know English, before he prepared his parcel for the post. He used to ask me: "What does Fox's paper, the *Morning Chronicle*, say of our emperor?" The last time I had to translate news for this officer from the English newspapers was about the beginning of July, 1808, a period when the attention of all Europe was attracted to the transactions taking place at Bayonne. I told him, not literally, but the simple facts, that General Savary had orders to bring Ferdinand VII, then the King of Spain, to Bayonne, there to be reprimanded by Napoleon in the presence of his father, King Charles the Fourth, for having usurped and robbed his parent, this venerable monarch, of his crown.

He was ordered by Napoleon to restore it forthwith—"or else."

No sooner said than done. Charles got back his crown, and feeling himself too feeble to bear the burden, he immediately abdicated in favour of the King of Naples; not the Bourbon branch, but the King Joseph Buonaparte. The newspaper I was translating added, Spain has now three kings, all absent; but the real sovereign of the country is reigning either at Seville or Cadiz, meaning the *Junta* chosen by the people. Those papers contained also articles about the Queen of Spain and Godoy, the Prince of the Peace.

It may be fairly asserted, that with the mutations of those kings, and the transfer of their realms, began Napoleon's worst difficulties. Soon after could be seen his Grand Army on its march to Spain, scarcely reposed from its fatigues and great victories in Germany and the Peace of Tilsit, to keep his brother Joseph on the throne of Spain, in spite of a nation composed of heroes and a determined people.

We were a long time without having any account of the Irish battalion at Madrid, when a *sous*-lieutenant, O'Moran, belonging to it, arrived at Flushing; he was threatened with insanity, and was ordered to the depot to repose himself. From him we learned a great deal that did not transpire before. Captain Fitzhenry was now the senior officer, to have a command when a detachment of troops from the legion should be ordered to Spain, which was hourly expected. We resolved, if possible, not to be sick when it came, at least not to be absent, either on leave or at the hospital. Captains O'Meally, Allen, Parrott and I agreed with Fitzhenry to hold ourselves ready to march at a minute's notice, we were all so desirous to get away from the bad climate of the isle of Walcheren, and to see more active service.

CHAPTER 4

Byrne's Guerrilla Fighting in Spain

In July, 1808, another battalion of the Irish legion, consisting of 600 men, left Flushing for Spain. Captain Fitzhenry, being the senior officer present, had the command, and joined at Pampeluna in September, 1808, the battalion which had retreated from Madrid with King Joseph. The latter being much reduced, the two battalions were incorporated into one under Fitzhenry, who was extremely active on this occasion, being recommended by Marshal Moncey and other generals, knowing well how to command, riding well—indeed, few could equal him in horsemanship, and he had two beautiful chargers. He was named *chef de bataillon* by a decree of the emperor dated 16th December, 1808.

Several other promotions were obtained at the same time: Edmond Saint-Leger, Miles Byrne (the author), John Allen, got their brevets as captains; Armand Parrott, Sheridan, Dolan, Malony, as lieutenants; Perry, Mac Egan, Keller, and Russell, as *sous*-lieutenants. These nominations completed the battalion in officers, which soon gained great praise for its instruction and discipline from Lieutenant-General Count de Buisson, Governor of Pampeluna.

Prince Berthier, who had been minister of war, was then with the emperor at Madrid, as chief of the staff, hearing the battalion so highly noted, and knowing the officers to be Irish exiled patriots, he ordered the battalion to make part of the army which marched against the English, then advancing into Spain, under the orders of General Sir John Moore; but after the defeat and death of this gallant general at Corunna, the battalion got orders to stop at Burgos, January, 1809, under the command of General Darmignac. The officers of that Irish battalion were much disappointed at not having been brought in contact with General Moore's army; many of them had fought against him in 1798, in the counties of Wexford and Wicklow in Ireland, when they were risking everything dear to them on earth to get rid of the cruel foreign yoke, by which the Irish were murdered and tortured beyond anything that ever took place in the most barbarous states of the world.

Yet General Moore had acquired a far higher reputation for humanity than different other generals of the English—Lake, for instance, who was commander-in-chief of the English at the Battle of Vinegar Hill. When Garrett Byrne of Ballymanus, on General Moore's word of honour, surrendered on condition to be allowed to expatriate himself for ever, this contract was faithfully executed, though Byrne was one of the principal leaders and chiefs throughout the insurrection; whilst his younger brother William, against whom no charge could be made, save that of using his influence to protect the English prisoners from bad treatment, was hanged and executed at Wicklow. Yet he had a written protection from General Lake, given to him by order of Lord Cornwallis.

Napoleon seeing that General Moore's rapid retreat on Corunna would deprive him of an opportunity of defeating an English Army, resolved to leave the further pacification to his brother King Joseph and the French marshals; he hastened back to Valladolid, and from thence to Burgos, where he arrived about eleven or twelve in the morning on the 17th of January, 1809, after making all the way on horseback, twenty-five leagues. The Irish battalion doing garrison duty at Burgos was apprised of the emperor's passage there, and was under arms at an early hour on the bridge to escort him to the bishop's palace, where he reposed himself for an hour and a half, and during his stay the Irish battalion mounted guard over him. Colonel Daniel O'Meara, who commanded the town of Burgos at the time under General Darmignac, was highly delighted that Napoleon had the Irish troops as his guard of honour; yet Colonel O'Meara was then unconnected with the Irish legion.

The emperor gave an audience and a good reception to the Spanish civil authorities at Burgos, whilst he refused to receive the ecclesiastical corps, which was very numerous, because they had no chief at their head to present them, their bishop being absent, and thought to be with the *Junta*.

The emperor started from Burgos in an open *caleche*, with General Savary, for Bayonne, where he arrived the same night: he was looking extremely well. It was the first time I had seen him since 1803, when he was First Consul, and he appeared to have become much stouter.

We were gratified to have been the only troops on guard during his short stay, and being conspicuously placed, and our uniforms tolerably good, we appeared to advantage. It was the first time that Napoleon had seen any part of that legion, which he so anxiously had organised in 1803, for the destined expedition to obtain the independence of Ireland, and to which he entrusted the honour of bearing his eagles, as he did to the French regiments of his guards. His subsequent decree to have the first Irish regiment of the legion organised into four war battalions and a depot is a proof of the good impression made on him by the battalion at Burgos, commanded by Fitzhenry.

A small advanced post on the road to Valladolid was commanded that day by an Irishman, Sergeant Mooney. The emperor, attracted by the green uniform of the soldiers, pulled up his horse to speak to the sergeant to enquire what regiment he belonged to, etc. Sergeant Mooney and his twelve men and a corporal were exceedingly vain of this interview, and used to boast of having been inspected by Napoleon himself in person.

General Darmignac was replaced in the command at Burgos, soon after the emperor's passage there, by Baron Thiébault, general of division, who was appointed also to be Governor of Old Castile. We were very glad to be under his orders, because he expressed himself on every occasion to be the friend of the exiled Irish, and he would often say to us:

If I am a general today, I owe, in a great measure, that rank and my rapid advancement to an Irishman, the unfortunate General O'Moran, who took me from the ranks of the volunteers in 1792, and had me named captain.

General Thiébault was highly educated and very well mannered, which was a great advantage to the troops under his command. He was the chief of the staff of that undaunted general, Junot, in Portugal, in 1808, and acquired great renown in his difficult situation; particularly at Lisbon, where he caused such improvements, in a very short space of time, by the sanitary changes which he obliged the inhabitants to make in their unclean city. At Burgos he took care to have the hospitals well provided with every necessary requisite for the convalescent. He took pleasure also in adding to the embellishment of a public walk, by the erection of a monument to the *Cid*. He had orders to commence the fort at Burgos, which became so famous in 1812, resisting all the assaults of the English Army commanded by Wellington.

Our soldiers were employed at the construction of that fort for a short time, in January, 1805, but the guerrilla war soon gave them other occupation, and the service became quite different to that we had to perform at Pampeluna, where we had to escort prisoners to Bayonne and to visit hospitals containing thousands of young soldiers sick with the "*maladie du pays.*" Here at Burgos, we had to escort the mail, or courier, coming from France to Madrid and returning, continually fighting with guerrillas, besides frequent disagreeable expeditions through the interior of the country. I shall mention a few of those that fell to my lot; and as every officer marched in his turn, it will show the busy service the battalion had to perform.

One night I was ordered to march, with a hundred and fifty men and two officers, Osmond and Malony, under the orders of the colonel of the 118th regiment, Duclos, who had an equal number of his own men. Just as we were setting out, Lieutenant Osmond was told that he was named to do the functions of *aide-de-camp* to the Prince of Isenberg, lately made General of Brigade in the French Army, and arrived at Burgos to get a command. I was sorry not to have Osmond with us, but I was glad he got a more agreeable situation; he was a good comrade and a distinguished officer.

Our sudden march was in consequence of a detachment of soldiers, who were sent to escort a number of cars loaded with bullets and ammunition from Valladolid to Aguilar-del-Campo, not arriving in this town in due time. Having no news whatever of them, Colonel Duclos was ordered to go in that direction to discover the reason. The sergeant who commanded the detachment, seeing the oxen not able to go further, went to a small village off the road, to lodge his men, and stop for the night. When he came to that village, there was not a living being to be found to give any information; all had fled. We, however, soon discovered, by the traces of blood through a field, where the eighteen bodies of the unfortunate French soldiers were buried, and in another field, a little distance off, where the cannon balls were sunk in a kind of marshy ground.

Colonel Duclos gave me an order to stop in a village near the one where the murders were perpetrated, till he could procure me cars to transport the bullets to the fort at Burgos. The second day I had sufficient, and I escorted the bullets and ammunition to Burgos, when General Thiébault told me that Colonel Duclos was called back to the command of his regiment, and the Adjutant-General Fontaine, who had been in Ireland with General Humbert, and whom I knew at Landernau in 1804, was appointed to replace him; that he wished me to command the troops of this moving column, as I had already a knowledge of the country.

After ten days' marching and counter-marching under the orders of Adjutant-General Fontaine, I was relieved by other troops, and I returned to Burgos to rejoin my battalion, and a few days after it was my turn to escort the mail to Lerma on the road to Madrid. A Mr. Murphy, of the house of Gordon & Murphy, of Madrid, availed himself of the escort to return to his home there; he was coming from France, where he had been detained as a prisoner of war, and he had an officer of *gendarmes* travelling in his coach with him to Madrid, where his presence was required to settle commercial business of the firm.

After King Joseph retreated from his capital in 1808, Mr. Murphy raised a regiment of cavalry at his own expense, and, when colonel at the head of it, fighting gallantly against Napoleon, he was taken prisoner and sent to France. Mr. Murphy was a very splendid looking man, very handsome, and a good Spanish patriot. Some of our officers experienced great kindness from him in 1807 at their camp in Madrid.

During our stay in Burgos, we had occasion to see several of the distinguished generals of the Republic and the Empire. One night I got an order to mount guard with my company over Marshal Lefebvre, Duke of Dantzic, who was returning to France. And after the siege of Saragossa, in February, 1809, the Duke of Montebello, Marshal Lannes, arrived with his staff, and his first *aide-de-camp* was Colonel Daniel O'Meara, who had been a captain and our comrade in the Irish legion in 1804, when we were on the coast near Brest, expecting to be sent to Ireland. William O'Meara met there his twin brother, Colonel Daniel O'Meara, who was the commander of the town of Burgos at the time.

The meeting of the brothers in a foreign land is another instance of the misfortunes of poor Ireland; had she been allowed to govern herself, those brave officers would have been an ornament to her commonwealth, in place of wandering abroad to seek their fortunes. Colonel William O'Meara was wounded beside Marshal Lannes, the day that hero was killed at the Battle of Essling, 1809. O'Meara was named Baron of the Empire and General of Brigade sometime after.

The Irish abroad, and particularly the exiles banished from their homes, were often more enthusiastic about celebrating St. Patrick's Day, than if they had been living quietly in the Green Island. This was the case with the officers of the Irish battalion at Burgos on the 17th March, 1809. We had a dinner party, to which we invited the commander of the place, Colonel Daniel O'Meara, and Colonel O'Neill, then a captain in the 47th regiment, formerly Walsh's, which had been commanded by his father, General O'Neill; his battalion had still several officers who had served in the brigades.

A Prussian regiment, newly formed, in the service of France, arrived in Burgos; one of the officers of it, a Mr. Plunkett, a very nice man, told us that his father was the son of an Irishman born in the Austrian States. We had also the sons of Irishmen who had served in the Irish regiments in the Spanish Army: Dalton, MacNalty, Cantan, etc. Thus, the exiles of 1798 had the honour of entertaining at the festival of their patron saint, Patrick, the descendants of those exiles of the different epochs of Ireland's sad history. What a picture an able hand might have drawn of Ireland's misfortunes, inspired by the varied and woeful histories of the ancestors of our guests! What a pity that the author of the *Exile of Erin* was not present at our dinner on St. Patrick's Day!

The guerrillas at this time (1809), though far from being organised as they were afterwards, gave great occupation to the French troops in the province of Old Castille. It became a very disagreeable service to be continually, night and day, marching to disperse those bands, and quite repugnant to our feelings, and we wished much to be brought to fight against a regular army; and I must say that Commandant Fitzhenry exerted himself greatly in this instance. And as soon as General Kellerman (son of Marshal Kellerman, the hero of Marengo), was given the command of an army corps, to co-operate with Marshal Soult and Marshal Ney against Sir Arthur Wellesley and the English, then thought to be about landing again in Portugal, and against the Spanish Army under the command of the Marquis de Romana, Fitzhenry's demand to have the honour for the Irish battalion of making part of the army was accorded.

The battalion was marched to Leon to make part of the army assembling then under General Kellerman for the expedition against the Marquis de Romana in the Asturias, and formed the advanced guard of the first brigade under General Chariot. On the 18th of May, 1809, the army left Leon, and had for several days to fight and force the passages in the mountains to Oviedo, until Romana's army was thought completely beaten and dispersed.

The battalion was then ordered to Gijon, a small seaport town, where we expected to stop for some time; but in consequence of Marshal Soult's retreat from Oporto, and Marshal Ney's from Galicia, General Kellerman had to evacuate the Asturias.

★★★★★★★★★★

We were delighted at the prospect of reposing ourselves a few days in the neat little town of Gijon. I was lodged at the house of a rich merchant on the quay, and I only found there one servant, a very old woman, who showed me my room. Her mistress, hearing that the strictest discipline was observed, sent me a message to say that she wished me to go to where she was hiding, at her gardener's house in the suburbs. I conducted this lady and her three children to their home. Captain Maguire called on me, and she politely invited him to come to dinner, which he accepted with pleasure, and we spent an agreeable evening with this amiable lady. The next morning, she told me that her husband, who was at their country place, a league or two from the town, wished her to bring a small escort for him, as he feared if he returned alone, he might fall into the hands of the patriots and be badly treated. She asked me to accompany her. Commandant Fitzhenry thought I could not refuse her, and bid me take a few men to serve as an escort. This lady had her horse and mule both saddled, and we were ready to start, when the drums beat to arms, fortunately for me, and in half an hour after the town was evacuated, and was only reoccupied the second day by a French battalion. I must say that this incident was a warning to me in all my future campaigns never to quit my battalion on any account.

★★★★★★★★★★

He ordered the Irish battalion on its way back to Burgos to pursue the division of the Marquis de Romana's army that had escaped into the mountains, and for several days the battalion, not more than six hundred strong, was attacking the rearguard of a division of several thousand At length the Spanish general, seeing but a small force following him, intended to attack in his turn and to draw the Irish battalion into an ambuscade; he was, however, soon put to flight again when General Chovel and his brigade, that had left Leon a few days before, came in sight. This general kept the Irish battalion with him in the mountains for some time, and then it returned to Leon, where the paymaster and the convalescents had remained.

There they met General Kellerman, who ordered them on another expedition through the mountains to Santandero, passing by Aguilar del Campo. Finally, the battalion returned to Burgos after a long absence, to be again under the orders of General Thiébault, who informed the officers that the emperor was so well pleased with the conduct of the Irish legion, that he decreed it should take the title of First Irish Regiment of the legion in the service of France, and ordered the Duke of Feltre, who was then minister of war, to have it organised with four war battalions, and a fifth with a depot which was placed the same year, June, 1809, at Landau, near the Rhine.

General Thiébault read at parade the new organisation, which was as follows:

Daniel O'meara, Colonel.
Peterzelli, *chef-de-bataillon*.   1st battalion at Flushing.
J. Fitzhenry,   *do.*   2nd   "   in Spain.
J. F. Mahony,   *do.*

       4th not yet formed.

Colonel O'Meara was ordered to remain at Landau to see the 3rd battalion completed and ready to march to Spain. Captain Lawless and the other five officers who were sent from the camp at Boulogne-sur-Mer to Brest in 1807 were ordered to Landau and placed in Commandant Mahony's battalion, Lawless as captain of grenadiers, but he soon received his brevet as "*chef*" of the 1st battalion, then at Flushing, with orders to repair there to replace Commandant Peterzelli (who was placed on General Monet's staff) in the command of that battalion. But before Lawless's arrival, the town was completely surrounded, by sea and land, by the English. He gallantly made his way through the enemy's fleet, in a small open boat, and got safe into the town and took the command of the battalion. There he distinguished himself in every sortie made against the enemy, till he received a dangerous wound, and most of his men were killed or wounded

General Monet having capitulated at Flushing without any stipulation for the Irish officers, Commandant Lawless thought it necessary to confide in the medical man of the place, Dr. Moke, in whose house he was, and who dressed his wounds and kept him in concealment till he was well enough, and found an opportunity of making his escape to Antwerp, where he brought the Eagle of the regiment and was received by Marshal Bernadotte (afterwards King of Sweden) with the highest marks of esteem and consideration for his brilliant conduct in the defence of Flushing. He was mentioned in the order of the army at Antwerp. The marshal having apprised the emperor of Commandant Lawless's escape, he ordered him to repair to Paris, where he conferred on him the decoration of the Legion of Honour and the rank of lieutenant-colonel.

Some of the officers of the Irish regiment being made prisoners at Flushing, and being taken to England, were there treated in every respect as French officers, no doubt from the fear of reprisals on the part of the French Government, had any violence been offered them.

Amongst the officers of the regiment who escaped to France and who were mentioned in the reports of the siege as having distinguished themselves, were Captains Barker, McCann, and Dowdall; the two latter died of their wounds at Ghent. Lieutenant Martin died of his wounds in some other town. Lieutenant O'Reilly, who escaped with Commandant Lawless, received the decoration of the Legion of Honour on arriving in France, for his brilliant conduct during the siege, and was soon named a captain in the 1st battalion, re-organised at Landau. Captain Tennant was named *commandant* in the room of Colonel Lawless.

The Duke of Feltre, receiving daily applications from Irishmen detained in the different depots of English prisoners in France to serve in the Irish regiment, thought proper to send an intelligent officer to these depots to ascertain that none but Irish should be allowed to take service. Captain Markey, who had been sent to Brest in 1807, was chosen for this purpose; he executed his mission with so much skill and activity, that after sending a great body of recruits to the Irish regiment, the Duke of Feltre took him for one of his *aides-de-camp*; in which situation he remained until he obtained the rank of lieutenant-colonel.

The 3rd battalion being completely organised in 1809 at Landau, was ordered to Spain under the command of Commandant Mahony; but in consequence of the disturbed state of Germany in the rear of the Grand Army, the battalion had to make several marches down the right bank of the Rhine before setting out for Spain, and only arrived at Burgos in the month of January, 1810, when it was united to the 2nd battalion.

Commandant Fitzhenry rose much in the estimation of the Governor of Old Castille after he returned with his battalion to Burgos, when all the details of our campaign in the Asturias under the command of General Kellerman were known. The latter ordered a gratification of one hundred *francs* to be given to each officer of his division; this money was the produce of a prize made at Gijon of an English ship laden with coffee and spices, and which was seized there and sold for the benefit of the hospitals. General Thiébault was not pleased to learn that the troops which were sent from his government of Old Castille, to make part of General Kellerman's division, did not participate in the gratification accorded to the officers. He asked Commandant Fitzhenry the cause of this omission, to which the latter mentioned his conversation on the subject with General Kellerman, which was simply this:

> *Commandant,* I have not comprised your officers for the gratification, knowing that they must have indemnified themselves in their long marches after the Marquis de Romana in in the interior of the Asturias.

Commandant Fitzhenry replied:

> General, the officers of the Irish battalion are men of high honour and principle, and I challenge and defy any Spaniard to come forward and prove that a single article or object was ever taken, save the regular rations ordered to be furnished to troops in campaign, by the officers of my battalion, etc.

It is true that General Kellerman did not pass for being the most agreeable chief to serve under. We were quitting his command and returning to Burgos. He wished to employ us on our way back there to disperse a part of Romana's army again rallying in the mountains. He could not have known the real force of the enemy we had to fight against, or he would have ordered more troops. We, however, manoeuvred in this critical situation much better than could have been expected.

One night that we had to stop in a poor village to give some repose to our men, Commandant Fitzhenry being lodged at the priest's house, got a great deal of important information from the venerable old clergyman of this parish all of which we found to be quite accurate and of infinite service to us next morning, and in consequence we avoided the ambuscade prepared for us by the Marquis de Romana; we turned his position and soon put his troops to flight. This short campaign in the Asturias gave us an opportunity of judging the character of its inhabitants, and I must say, that though in time of war, we were generally on friendly terms with them.

I was one day ordered by General Chovel to command a detachment of troops to escort a Spanish agent who was going to a village six leagues off, to procure provisions for headquarters. We arrived there in the night. The agent took his billet at the *alcade's* house, and I was lodged at the parish priest's. This clergyman was middle aged, and very well looking. The next morning, whilst the Spanish agent, acting in the name of King Joseph, was regulating with the senor *alcade* about the quantity and nature of the provisions to be got ready, I had a long and interesting conversation with my host. This worthy patriotic ecclesiastic told me he had studied at Salamanca, and had been acquainted there with many of my countrymen, both students of the Irish College, and officers of the Irish regiment in the Spanish service; he added, that he thought there was a great similitude in many respects between the people of our respective countries, their sufferings, etc.

I answered there could be no comparison, as in his country, at that moment, the inhabitants were not persecuted and deprived of their civil rights on account of the religion they professed. I allowed, however, that the Spaniards had suffered in their disastrous wars on account of the monarchs imposed on them: one time from an Austrian branch, another from the house of the Bourbons of France, and then from the Buonaparte family: whilst in poor Ireland the millions of unemancipated Catholic serfs were kept in bondage by a Protestant ascendancy of a few hundred thousand individuals, acting there the part of the cruel taskmasters for England. That in changing the Spanish dynasties, no religious persecutions took place in Spain.

I perfectly agreed with him that the Spaniards had a right to govern themselves and to choose the form of government they wished; whilst, on the other hand, I maintained that no matter who the chief of the French Government was, he became responsible to the nation to take the best means to secure the friendship of the neighbouring states, and their perfect neutrality in time of war; that it could never be forgotten, that after the revolution of 1789, when hostilities began, Protestant Prussia and Catholic Spain were the first powers to attack and invade France.

To be sure, other powers soon followed the example, as Protestant England and Catholic Austria; the latter on the Rhine and on the Alps; the former got possession of Toulon by treachery, and made a bold attempt to take Dunkirk, but that town was commanded by an Irishman, O'Meara, and the Duke of York and the English Army under his orders were forced to make a shameful retreat.

Again, in 1806, had the Battle of Iena been lost by France, your King Charles the Fourth was prepared to declare war against her. Now, under all those circumstances, a sure guarantee was required by the French Government from the Spanish nation:

I am far from pretending that the right means were taken to secure it.

In the most animated tone did this Spanish priest reply, not as I expected indeed, to my observations. He said:

Sir, don't think that it is because we want Ferdinand more than Joseph, that the war is carried on against you; it is because we want to remain a Spanish nation independent of foreigners, and we hope it will never cease until the last French soldier is driven from our country. You are here in a province, the Asturias, which the Moors could not conquer, and, with God's help, you shall fail also.

I could not help admiring the patriotism of this enthusiastic ecclesiastic: he reminded me of the virtuous clergymen who suffered torture and death as martyrs, both in the field and on the scaffold, in Ireland in 1798, endeavouring to set their country free from the cruel foreign yoke. Historians writing on the wars of that period seem to disapprove the part some Irish clergymen took in them, whilst they admire the Spaniards fighting against Catholic France. Be that as it may, the names of the priests and monks who were buried under the ruins of Saragossa, in the month of February, 1809, will be revered and remembered in that country to the end of time; as sure as that the names of Father Roche, Father Redmond, the two Fathers Murphy, and Father Kearns will never be forgotten in the county of Wexford as long as the Slaney runs into the sea!

One of the Fathers Murphy was killed at the Battle of Arklow, on the 9th of June, 1798. The other four were hanged and quartered in the most disgusting and cruel manner, and died martyrs to their country's cause. With three of them I was on the most intimate terms, all through the insurrection, *viz*.: Fathers John Murphy, Kearns and Roche. As to poor Father Redmond, he was the curate of our parish, and it was he who attended my dear father in his last moments in 1797. Father Frank Kavanagh was the parish priest, and they had three chapels in the parish, Clough, Crane and Monaseed, to attend on Sundays. Father Redmond took no part whatever in the war; he resided quite retired, with his family, in the neighbourhood of Earl Mountnorris' mansion.

One day a detachment from our camp being sent there to procure some provisions, Father Redmond presented himself to them, and in the most humble manner beseeched them not to burn or plunder the concerns of the earl, who was one of the best of men. He succeeded in his request and retired again to his home, where he remained till the war was over, when Lord Mountnorris had him arrested and escorted to the English camp at Gorey Hill with a rope about his neck. There he had him hanged from the bough of a tree; and whilst he was suspended, the noble earl had the courage to discharge his case of pistols through the body of this innocent priest, whose only crime was that of having contributed to save the premises of that cowardly earl, who wanted to redeem his lost reputation by this cruel murder. He knew he was censured for not being at the head of his corps of yeoman cavalry, when they fought and were defeated on the 26th of May, 1798. His lieutenants, Busky and Swan, were killed, and almost all the men.

CHAPTER 5

Sieges of Astorga and Ciudad Rodrigo

The Emperor Napoleon, after the Battle of Wagram and his other victories in Germany, heard the unpleasant news of the capitulation of the French garrison at Flushing to the English on the 15th of August, 1809; and knowing that the 1st battalion of the Irish regiment, commanded by William Lawless, made part of that garrison, he gave orders to have another 1st battalion forthwith organised at Landau, the depot where the men and officers were assembled for its formation. Captain John Tennant was promoted to the command of it, with the rank of *chef de bataillon*, in the room of Commandant Lawless, who was reported killed during the siege of Flushing. (It was in November he escaped to Antwerp.)

Lieutenant Osmond, who had been employed as *aide-de-camp* for a short time in Spain, to the Prince Isenberg, received his commission as captain adjutant-major to Commandant Tennant's battalion; and, indeed, a better choice could not have been made. MacCarthy, a volunteer in a French regiment at the camp of Boulogne-sur-Mer in 1804, got rapid promotion: he was a lieutenant at the Battle of Wagram, where he distinguished himself, and for this he was named knight of the Legion of Honour and captain of grenadiers to the 1st battalion of the Irish regiment at Landau, commanded by Tennant. MacCarthy was a fine officer, highly instructed, and the best of comrades.

Besides the Captains O'Quin, Markey, Magrath, de Meyers, etc., the 1st battalion was composed of lieutenants and sublieutenants of worth, and all were animated with a military spirit that could not be surpassed in any regiment; such were, the youngest Saint-Leger, O'Brien, Berthemy, Lynch, Magrath, junior; young Osmond, nephew to the captain; Swanton, Wall, junior, Glashan, senior, MacAuley, Markey's nephew, etc., etc.

How disagreeable and discouraging it must have been to these young officers to witness the injudicious manner the Minister of War, Feltre, behaved towards them. They at least expected that when the place of captain became vacant in the regiment, it would be filled by the senior lieutenant or by one chosen by the chiefs, as is the case in the French regiments. One instance will suffice to prove the contrary was the case in the Irish regiment. General Clark, when he was Governor of Berlin in 1806, became acquainted there with a Mr. Ferguson, a Scotch gentleman.

In 1809, General Clark, then Duke of Feltre, and Minister of War at Paris, was waited on and solicited by his former acquaintance, Mr. Ferguson, for some situation under the French Government. The minister immediately granted him the commission of captain in the Irish regiment, to the prejudice of all those brave lieutenants before mentioned. No doubt, Mr. Ferguson was a well-bred gentleman, but he was more than fifty years of age, and he had not the least idea of the military profession, as he candidly owned himself to Marshal Massena in Spain, who took compassion on him, and gave him permission to go and stop at Valladolid until an opportunity to return to the depot of the Irish regiment at Landau should occur.

Many other instances occurred of old captains (who should have been retired) being put at the head of companies in the Irish regiment by the Duke of Feltre, who did not seem to feel for the military spirit and emulation, which is the life and soul of an army. His depriving those brave young officers of the advancement they were so well entitled to, and appointing men to situations who had no claims as Irish patriots, showed that the Duke of Feltre cared little about the independence of Ireland; and, indeed, he could not have given a better proof than that of having named John Francis Mahony *chef de bataillon* over the heads of such captains as Lawless, Tennant, Markey, Brangan, O'Malley, Saint-Leger, Allen, Ware, etc.

Mahony had nothing to recommend him to hold a rank in an Irish regiment in the French service: he emigrated as a sub-lieutenant in 1792, took service in England and served in Egypt against the French in 1799; after the Peace of Amiens in 1802 he sold out his commission in the English Army and returned to France. He never asked to be employed so long as any hopes of an expedition to Ireland was entertained. In 1809 he was named to command the 3rd battalion of the Irish regiment, which was ordered to Spain, to join the 2nd battalion at Burgos. But what was still worse, was, not to have promoted the senior superior officer of the regiment to the rank of colonel of it.

Had Commandant Fitzhenry got the situation, Captain Ware would have replaced him, and the first lieutenant would have been named captain in his place; and promotion would thus have been obtained down to the soldiers in the ranks.

Colonel Daniel O'Meara, whom we knew in 1809 as commander of the place at Burgos, was named colonel of the first Irish regiment the same year, and ordered to the depot at Landau, to have the war battalions organised and equipped, ready to march against the enemies of France. Unfortunately, though a brave and an honourable man, he was quite unfit for the task of commanding a regiment; having been mostly employed on the staff, he knew little of the evolutions or manoeuvres of infantry, and he was getting too old to learn, and being addicted to drinking, he was rendered not only useless but unsafe at the head of his regiment.

He remained at the depot, waiting till the 3rd battalion, arrived in Spain, should be united with the 2nd, to go and take the command of both. But, as is mentioned in the last chapter, Commandant Mahony had to march with his battalion for some time down the Rhine, to disperse guerrillas that were attempting to make a diversion in the rear of the French Grand Army, and interrupting all small detachments, which might have become formidable and dangerous had the Germans possessed the same kind of spirit and talents for a guerrilla war that the Spaniards had. In consequence of this short excursion on the Rhine, the 3rd battalion only reached Burgos in January, 1810, after its long march in winter.

I was truly glad to see it arrive, as I met amongst the officers composing it several of my former friends and comrades: first of all, Captain Paul Murray, whose acquaintance I made in the mountains of the county of Wicklow in 1798, at a memorable period of Ireland's sad history; next, Captain Brangan, who was destined to have taken an active part in poor Robert Emmet's unsuccessful undertaking in 1803. My acquaintance with Jackson, Bourke, Delany, Nugent, Cabour de la Haye (the nephew of the illustrious General Foy), only commenced at Burgos in 1810, and I must say, for the latter, I never knew a more upright, better, or braver man than he was all the time he remained in the Irish regiment; and to his last moment, when he was colonel of the staff, and enjoying influence, his great pleasure was to ascertain how he could be useful to his former comrades. All his acts were in perfect harmony with those of his uncle, General Foy.

As to Jackson and Bourke, they were young men of ability, for whom I had the sincerest friendship till death and banishment separated us. Captain Bourke was killed on the 29th of August, 1813, at Lowenberg on the Bober. Captain Jackson was banished from France on a ministerial order of the war minister, the Duke of Feltre, in 1815, as a Buonapartist, without any trial or proof. He went to South America, where he soon obtained the rank of colonel, fighting for the independence of his newly-adopted country.

Young Delany was brother to the gentleman I met at Mr. Emmet's in 1803, and was the friend of poor Thomas Russell and of his nephew by marriage, William Hamilton.

Captain Ferguson looked rather conspicuous, being well mounted on a white pony, and riding every day on the march beside his company, the command of which he left to his lieutenant, as he had not yet had time to learn the words of command before setting out from the depot at Landau. At table, however, in the evening, he was a perfect gentleman, and Commandant Mahony seemed to appreciate that military quality in one of his captains, being an excellent judge himself of the etiquette to be observed on such occasions, from his experience at the mess tables of the English officers whilst he remained in that service.

Commandant Mahony would have been rather well looking but for a squint which he had, and which gave him at times a mean air; particularly so on account of the impediment he had in his speech: his stammer would often prevent him uttering a word for half a minute, and then his face was distorted to a most extraordinary degree. He, however, could command without stammering and sing also with ease.

I need not say that we received Commandant Mahony and his officers of the 3rd battalion at dinner, and entertained them in the best way we could the day they arrived, and that we spent a very pleasant evening together, talking over old times.

The two battalions being united, the *sous-intendant militaire* inspected them and classed the officers. Captain O'Malley passed to the 3rd battalion in the first class. Captain Murray replaced him in the 2nd battalion. Joseph Parrott was named adjutant-major to the 3rd battalion with Commandant Mahony. At this review, in the absence of Colonel O'Meara, Commandant Fitzhenry, as senior superior officer, took the command of the Irish regiment then at Burgos.

The general of division, Solignac, replaced General Thiébault as Governor of Old Castille. He employed the 2nd battalion in all his expeditions against the Marquis Ceto Porlier and the other Spanish chiefs, which made a great name for Fitzhenry and the officers who composed that battalion. Captain Allen, with his company of *voltigeurs*, surprised, near Najara, in the night, a squadron of Spanish cavalry, consisting of four officers and forty men. After taking horses that were fit for service, General Solignac had the rest sold and the money distributed amongst Captain Allen's *voltigeurs*, to reward them for their activity. This had an excellent effect on the men of the regiment.

The Irish regiment was relieved in Old Castille, where it had been constantly engaged in expeditions against the guerrillas, by the Young Imperial Guards arriving from France in February, 1810. At this time orders were given for the formation of the eighth corps, under General Junot, Duke of Abrantes. It was composed of three divisions, commanded by Lieutenants-Generals Clausel, Solignac, and Lagrange.

The Irish regiment made a part of the 2nd division, General Solignac's, in the 2nd brigade, commanded by General Thomier. On the first of March, 1810, it left Burgos for Rio Seco, and here Colonel O'Meara arrived from the depot at Landau, with a detachment, and took the command of the regiment. At Rio Seco the division was united and formed the headquarters of Generals Solignac and Thomier for some days.

The Duke of Abrantes had his headquarters with the division Lagrange at Valladolid.

The division of Clausel blockaded Astorga and began to make a regular siege; but his division was relieved in the trenches by General Solignac's, and he marched to the advanced posts before the English to prevent them raising the siege. The 2nd division encamped near the town, and the Irish regiment was employed day and night in the trenches during this memorable siege, which lasted three weeks.

On the 19th of April, 1810, the general-in-chief, the Duke of Abrantes, arrived, and as the Spanish garrison would not surrender, he ordered the breach to be made, which with great difficulty was effected on the 21st of April, 1810. A battalion of chosen troops was organised to mount the breach, and Captain Allen's company of *voltigeurs*, consisting of 150 men of the 2nd battalion of the first Irish regiment, marched at its head. After Captain Allen received his instructions as he passed the Duke of Abrantes in the trenches, he divided his company into two sections, and at the head of the first he marched on to the breach.

At 5 o'clock p.m., when the signal was given, he had to pass more than 200 yards uncovered before he got to the bottom of the breach, under the fire of above two thousand men; he, however, mounted it with such bravery and decision, that when he arrived at the top, he turned round and saluted the general and the army of above 30,000 men; then pointing to his men to fire on the enemy that was on his flank, and to follow him into the town, he took possession of a house near the rampart, according to the instructions of the Duke of Abrantes, in order to keep up the communication between the breach and the trenches; and this he defended the whole night.

In order to facilitate the mounting of the breach to the rest of the battalion, he made a temporary rampart of the men's sacks on his left flank, from behind which he kept up a continual fire on the enemy that approached the breach from the rampart, who he feared might cut off his communication with the trenches. All the officers, senior to Allen, of the battalion being killed or wounded, all orders were given by him during the night till the arrival of Captain Legrave, *aide-de-camp* to the Duke of Abrantes, who had been designed to command the battalion, but who did not join it till one in the morning.

A drummer of Captain Allen's, in mounting the breach, had both his legs broken, but he kept his drum, sat down and beat the charge as long as he was able, and indeed until all the battalion got up: for this he received the cross of the Legion of Honour. The rest of Commandant Fitzhenry's battalion remained all night near the breach, ready to mount the first in the morning, and suffered much. Every company had men killed and wounded, carrying ladders to the breach, which was scarcely practicable. His adjutant-major Perry, and his adjutant Gougie were both wounded, the latter lost his arm.

The battalion received on this occasion great praise from the Duke of Abrantes and the other generals. Captain Allen's conduct was so remarkable as to excite general admiration throughout the army assembled there: indeed, it exceeded all praise that could be given him. The Duke of Abrantes, who was so brave himself and such an admirer of heroic actions, was heard to exclaim:

Good heavens! I would give two thousand *napoleons* to see that brave man alive in the morning; but it is impossible for him to escape under such a tremendous fire.

The garrison seeing no chance of retaking the breach, which was steadily defended by Captain Allen during the night, sent a flag of truce at daylight to the general-in-chief and surrendered at discretion. Five thousand fine troops marched out and laid down their arms on the glacis, and the Irish regiment was ordered to escort them to Valladolid, which was considered a very hard service after all the fatigue they had endured day and night in the trenches during the siege.

After the town surrendered, Captain Allen was ordered to return by the breach, as an honour, with the remains of the battalion, which was reduced to about 150 men out of 900, the rest being all killed or wounded. The general-in-chief, Junot, Duke of Abrantes, accompanied by all the generals present, Solignac, Lagrange, Thomier, Sainte-Croix, etc., came to review those brave men who remained of the battalion that had mounted the breach. Nothing could equal the expressions of admiration and praise. Each embraced Captain Allen, the only captain who had escaped. Captain Allen and the remains of his company was sent into Astorga after it had surrendered, to wait the return of the rest of the Irish regiment sent to escort the prisoners to Valladolid. Colonel O'Meara of the Irish regiment was named to command the place, and the greatest order and discipline was kept up, no sort of plunder being allowed.

The Irish regiment returned to Astorga after having escorted the prisoners to Valladolid, and in the beginning of May, being relieved by a Swiss regiment at Astorga, they joined the division of General Solignac and marched to Toro.

It was during this march that the general-in-chief the Duke of Abrantes placed Colonel O'Meara on the staff of General Solignac, and gave the command of the Irish regiment to Commandant Fitzhenry. At the same time Generals Solignac and Thomier having assembled the officers of the 3rd battalion of the Irish regiment in the presence of Commandant Mahony, and hearing their complaints against him, he was attached to the duke's staff, and the command of the 3rd battalion given to Captain Allen in his stead.

Captain Allen felt on this occasion that he could not command a battalion in which there were two captains senior to him; but General Thomier told him it was the wish of the Duke of Abrantes, and that he ought to comply, as the duke expected by every courier his brevet as *chef de bataillon*.

The regiment was ordered from Toro to Salamanca in the beginning of June, 1810, in which town Prince Massena had just arrived to take the command of the three corps of army destined to invade Portugal. The 2nd corps was commanded by General Regnier, the 6th by Marshal Ney, and the 8th by Junot, Duke of Abrantes. The latter assembled the Irish officers on their arriving at Salamanca, to announce to them the promotions and decorations that were just arrived from Paris for the regiment. He expressed great regret that Captain Allen's brevet as *chef de bataillon* was not amongst them, but promised him he would never cease his endeavours till he obtained his brevet from the Duke of Feltre, then Minister of War. Captain Allen resumed the command of his company of *voltigeurs* in the 2nd battalion, and Captain O'Malley, the senior captain of the 3rd battalion, took the command of it.

The 6th corps commanded by Marshal Ney was employed to make the siege of Ciudad Rodrigo, and the 8th corps commanded by Junot, Duke of Abrantes, marched in the beginning of June, 1810, from Salamanca to the advanced posts before the English, and occupied the line between Almeida and Ciudad Rodrigo.

A *battalion d'élite*, or chosen troops of the Irish regiment, was assembled to act at the advanced posts during the siege, and Captain Ware of the grenadiers of the 2nd battalion of the Irish was named by the Duke of Abrantes to command it. In an attack made on a division of advanced posts by General Sainte-Croix and his brigade of cavalry, seconded by Captain Ware, the English were driven back under the walls of Almeida and the Fort of Conception. Captain Ware was highly complimented by all the generals for the brilliant conduct of his battalion during this action. He received at this time his brevet of *chef de bataillon* for the 4th battalion of the Irish regiment, then forming at Landau in France, to which town he was ordered to repair without delay. He was ordered to give up the command of his company of grenadiers to Captain Byrne of the 2nd battalion, (the author.)

At the end of July, 1810, as soon as Ciudad Rodrigo surrendered, the Irish regiment went with the Duke of Abrantes to his headquarters at Ledesma, in which place it remained until the camp was formed at Saint-Félix-le-Grand. From this camp it went to be employed at the siege of Almeida until the town was blown up and surrendered in the end of August the same year. After this siege, Massena, with the three army corps, marched into Portugal, and the Irish regiment, being considered as light troops, always marched at the head of General Thomier's brigade.

This brave general seemed happy to have them under his command in entering Portugal, and in an energetic and eloquent speech which he made to the officers of the Irish regiment the morning of the Battle of Busaco, at the moment he expected the order for attacking the English, he reminded them of all the wrongs of unfortunate Ireland, and called also to their recollection Fontenoy, where the Irish

Brigade in the service of France decided the battle.

The day after the Battle of Busaco, the 8th corps marched on Coimbra and completely turned the left wing of the English Army, then in full retreat on Lisbon. The Irish regiment shared in the honour of this day, and indeed in every place where the English attempted to resist, until they were driven behind their intrenchments at Torres Vedras, near Lisbon.

The Irish regiment encamped at the most advanced posts, within cannon shot of the enemy's line, and remained in this position until the army was ordered to fall back on Santarem and Torres Novas in December, 1810. It was detached with General Thomier in a small village called Praseras, where the companies *d'élite* were continually employed endeavouring to find provisions, which now became very difficult to procure. It became necessary to go out into the enemy's line and there to fight and run the greatest dangers; but the privations of this memorable campaign are too generally known for it to be necessary to say more than that the Irish regiment bore them with as much fortitude as any other regiment in the army.

They were for nearly eight months without pay or rations, except at Torres Vedras, where the regiment came on the first of January, 1811, to be on service with the general-in-chief, Prince Massena. In this place, goat's flesh was distributed once a week; an ounce to each man, with some maize or indian corn; but even this scanty allowance ceased.

About the end of February, 1811, several regiments were ordered to send into France the officers, sergeants and corporals of their 3rd battalions, and to leave the private men to be incorporated in the 1st and 2nd battalions, or war battalions. Captain Parrott conducted the officers and Sergeants and corporals of the 3rd battalion of the Irish regiment to Landau.

On the 1st of March, previous to the retreat, the Duke of Abrantes marched forward to attack the English, or rather to manoeuvre on their line. The Irish regiment left Torres Novas and accompanied him on this expedition, during which he was wounded. The regiment returned from the advanced posts to Torres Novas on the 6th of March; on which day the retreat began on the whole line. General Solignac's division, in which was the Irish regiment, covered the retreat for several days, until the army was concentrated at Pombal, at which place Marshal Ney got the command of the rearguard of the army; and as every regiment furnished a battalion for the extreme rear guard, the Irish battalion had this honour frequently during the retreat, which lasted nearly a month before the army reached the Spanish frontier; never making more than three or four leagues a day, and continually fighting.

The Irish battalion was reviewed at Celerico, near the frontiers of Spain, by the general, who was highly pleased to see still so many men present. At this town Marshal Ney left the army and returned to France.

By an order of the division, an officer from each regiment was sent into Spain to provide shoes and other articles to be ready for the men by the time they should get to their cantonments in Spain. Captain Allen, who was sent from the Irish regiment on this mission, left Ciudad Rodrigo on the 26th of March, 1811, accompanied by the colonel of the 22nd regiment and several other officers. They were attacked by the guerrillas, and the adjutant of the 22nd was taken prisoner, as was Captain Allen, after receiving two wounds on his head. After enduring the most cruel treatment, they were escorted to Cadiz, where they remained as prisoners for eighteen months. The Duke of Abrantes was quite enraged when he heard of Captain Allen's misfortune, and expressed the greatest sorrow on the occasion.

After Marshal Ney left the army at Celerico, General Loiseau took the command of the 6th corps. The army manoeuvred to the left by Guarda Bellemonte. On the 1st of April it heard of the birth of the King of Rome. The 2nd corps, commanded by General Regnier, had to sustain a desperate attack on the 3rd of April from the English and Portuguese. On the 5th of April the army arrived on the Spanish frontier, passing Alfaetas, and on the 6th and 7th encamped near Rodrigo. On the 8th the army passed by the town, took biscuit for four days to bring them to the neighbourhood of Toro and Salamanca and other cantonments, to recover the fatigues and privations of the campaign.

The Irish battalion marched with the army for about two leagues from Ciudad Rodrigo, on the road to Salamanca, when Commandant Fitzhenry received an order to return with his battalion to make part of the garrison of Rodrigo. He desired the senior captain (O'Malley), to take the command and to return with the battalion, whilst he himself rode on to the head of the column to get permission to go to Salamanca, which was granted him by the general.

The battalion returned immediately to Rodrigo, and was inspected on the glacis by the governor, General Rheno, who told the men that he had still plenty of provisions for them, notwithstanding all that had been delivered to the army passing by; and certainly, he kept his word, and did everything that depended on him to console the soldiers for their disappointment at not getting to the fine cantonments at Toro. On entering the town, every man got a loaf of fine white bread, the first they had tasted for several months, and a ration of meat and wine. This, with being tolerably well lodged, made both officers and men soon forget the miseries they had suffered in the severe campaign of Portugal.

The service of the place was hard enough, there being only two battalions, one of the 15th regiment and one of the Irish, and the town being nearly blockaded by the enemy as soon as the army had gone to its cantonments. The cattle which was for the provision of the garrison, being sent to graze, was, with a number of the officers' horses, servants, etc., taken by the Spanish cavalry, and marched off so suddenly that the garrison was not able to overtake them. The governor, after firing a few cannon shots, to no purpose, ordered the drawbridges to be raised and the gates to be shut, and at nine o'clock at night, 300 of the Irish battalion, and 300 of the 15th regiment were marched out and ordered to surround a village about four leagues off, where he suspected the enemy would halt for the night with their booty.

At daylight the village was attacked, and the cattle, horses, servants, etc., retaken, with four Spanish officers and the principal part of the detachment under their orders, all of whom were brought to Rodrigo before twelve o'clock the following day. One of these officers was allowed by the governor to write to his chief to say that he and another would be exchanged for Captain Allen; but unfortunately, the latter was already sent off a prisoner to Cadiz.

The English and Portuguese forces being occupied with the blockade of Almeida, and preparing to besiege that town, which had but a feeble garrison of 1,500 men, commanded by the brave General Brenier, the Governor of Rodrigo was enabled to send different detachments to bring in provisions for the troops of the garrison there. In every excursion of the kind the Irish were employed in their turn, if not sometimes preferred by General Rheno, under whose orders they served with the utmost zeal and fidelity.

On the 18th of April, 1811, Commandant Fitzhenry, who had obtained permission to remain a few days at Salamanca, received orders to return to Rodrigo to join his battalion, and to bring with him all the men of the regiment who were convalescent and able to march. He set out on the 19th with about 70 men; on the 22nd of April, after passing Ledesma, he and his detachment were taken prisoners by Don

Julian and his band of above a thousand strong. The wife of a soldier who made part of the detachment escaped and brought the news to the battalion.

At the end of April, the remains of the different corps of Prince Massena's army received orders to get provisions for several days, and on the 30th of April and 1st of May to march to Rodrigo. On the 3rd of May, the 2nd, 6th, 8th and 9th corps, with a part of the Imperial cavalry under the orders of Marshal Bessières, Duke of Istria, were reviewed by the commander-in-chief Massena, on the plain near Ciudad Rodrigo. The Irish battalion passed the review with its brigade.

On the 4th of May the army marched in three columns towards Almeida, and early on the 5th attacked the English and Allied Army. The battle continued all day with various chances of success, until Massena found means at night to give orders to the Governor of Almeida, General Brenier, to blow up the fortifications; after the execution of which he was to fight his way across the English Army. This brave general, with his garrison of 1,500 men, punctually performed his instructions, and fought at their head the whole night through the English lines, and at daylight he arrived in sight of the French line, and was soon supported by the second corps under the command of General Regnier, whose advanced posts were at Saint-Felix.

On the 6th and 7th, the army was ordered to return to their cantonments, and a new organisation was ordered to take place. The different corps, then greatly reduced, were to form six divisions, to be called the Army of Portugal, and the command of it to be given to Marshal Marmont, Duke of Ragusa, who had just come to replace Massena in the command of the army. General Foy commanded the 1st division.

General Brenier, for his brilliant conduct, got his brevet of lieutenant-general and the command of the 6th division of the Army of Portugal. The Irish battalion made part of his division, with the 22nd, 65th and 17th Léger regiment and the Hanoverian legion.

Further Details of Captain Allen's Brilliant Services.

General Solignac being in pursuit of the enemy at the town of Najara in the beginning of February, 1810, desired Commandant Fitzhenry to send him three captains of his battalion; Ware, Allen and I were ordered: the general told us we should have to march in the night with our companies, on three separate roads, to surround a small town four or five leagues off, where a numerous corps of the enemy's

Battle of Fuente d'Onoro, 5th May, 1811

cavalry had taken up their quarters. We got three sure guides, and ten o'clock at night marched on this fatiguing expedition. At daylight, Ware and I met, after our men had blockaded the ways leading out of the town. We feared that Allen had met impediments, as he was not arrived in sight of the place.

We apprised the authorities of our mission, and the *alcade* of the town hastened to come and inform us that the corps of cavalry left his town at midnight; he showed us the street by which it took its departure; he could not tell us more, except that it was formidable, to which we paid little attention, knowing that their policy was to exaggerate in such cases. Ware and I hastened to get refreshments for our soldiers, and we then returned by the road which Allen should have come by, had he not met some obstacles by the way; but before we marched two leagues, our anxiety was relieved; we reached the village where he had made the corps of cavalry prisoners, and he was on his way back, escorting them to headquarters, and had arrived here several hours before we did.

In the trenches at the siege of Astorga, previous to the breach being mounted, Captain Ware seeing by the order of the day that his company of grenadiers was not to march at the head of the battalion designed for the attack, came to claim his right to that post. General Solignac, whom he addressed on the subject, immediately said to the Duke of Abrantes, who was just by: "The captain of grenadiers of the 2nd battalion of the Irish regiment claims as his right to be the first to mount the breach."

To which the duke mildly replied, "Captain, have I not the right to order the dispositions for the attack? You will be with your battalion and its chief, Fitzhenry, at the foot of the breach to assure our success. I have given this order knowing well I could count on you."

Captain Ware retired, when the duke said, "It is cheering and augurs well to receive reclamations of that nature and at such a moment. I suppose, General Solignac, you know that captain well."

"Certainly, Monsieur le Duc, he accompanied me in all my expeditions, night and day, in Old Castille, and I have recommended him in consequence of his brilliant conduct in these affairs and combats to the Minister of War for advancement, to which he is so well entitled, as indeed I must say, all the officers of Fitzhenry's battalion are; unfortunately, these brave men have to wait till vacancies for promotion occur in their own regiment." (As yet the second Irish regiment was not organised.)

Our general of brigade, Thomier, was pleased to speak in the highest terms of the regiment since it made part of his brigade: he alluded to the coolness of the officers in the moments of peril, as well as to their bravery and exactitude in performing and conforming to all military duties, etc.

Three days previous to this conversation with the Duke of Abrantes, Captain Allen, returning to our camp from the trenches, where he had been on guard for twenty-four hours with his company, crossing a field considered quite beyond the reach of the guns of the rampart, had two of his soldiers killed by his side: their heads were cut off by a cannon ball, and Allen's uniform bespattered with their blood and brains. He instantly gave the command to his *voltigeurs* to disperse as riflemen through the fields, and in this way, he reached the camp without further loss, though several volleys were instantly fired at him and his men.

General Thomier, who witnessed Allen's prompt decision on this occasion in dispersing his men, as the best way to save them from the twenty-four pounders on the rampart, mentioned this circumstance to the general-in-chief Junot, which probably was the reason that he appointed Allen to lead and mount the breach, seeing he was a man of character and decision in perilous situations, and indeed he judged him rightly.

I never felt greater pleasure, or was more agreeably surprised than when Allen's confidential soldier came to me in the night at the foot of the breach to say that his captain hoped I would be able to send him something to drink, for there was no water to be had in the house where they were. It was the first news I had that poor Allen had escaped. I brought this brave soldier immediately to General Thomier, who was equally rejoiced; and he went himself to apprize the Duke of Abrantes of Allen's situation, and wonderful good luck in escaping alive after such fighting.

When it was ascertained that Captain Allen had taken possession of a house in the town, near the rampart, which he resolved to defend during the night, and that he was able to preserve his communication open with the breach, a detachment of our regiment was ordered to bring him refreshments for his brave soldiers. Young Delany, a *sous*-lieutenant, had the command of the men carrying the provisions to Captain Allen's troops.

He succeeded in getting over the breach and in delivering carefully all the articles that were entrusted to his charge, and he recrossed the breach at the head of his detachment, to rejoin his battalion; but he had several of his men killed and wounded, and he himself had a musket ball through his arm. He went to the place in the trenches, where our surgeon was busy dressing the wounds by candle-light, and he sat down on a bank of clay, looking on for some time, when Surgeon Prevost happened to turn his head and perceived him.

He said, "Lieutenant Delany, I beg your pardon, but my instructions are to oblige all those who come here conducting or carrying the wounded men, to return forthwith to their respective companies, and I am nor to allow anyone to remain here but those who want to have their wounds examined and dressed."

"Well, I would thank you to examine my wound," replied Delany.

"How!" exclaimed the surgeon, "my positive instructions are to dress the officers' wounds first, and you have said nothing to me, though you have been there looking on for more than half an hour."

"Oh! I am in no hurry; the poor soldiers, whose wounds you have been dressing, stood in more need of your assistance than I did."

As soon as Lieutenant Delany had his arm dressed and tied up, he rejoined his company, and would not avail himself of his wound to retire to the camp.

In Surgeon Prevost's detailed report to the general-in-chief upon the different cases of the wounded he had been dressing during the night, he mentioned the humane forbearance of one of the Irish officers, which circumstance caused pleasure and delight to the brave and intrepid General Junot, who used often to speak of it and to say, "What a pity such men have not a country of their own to fight for!"

A white flag, or flag of truce, was perceived at daybreak on the ramparts, and immediately the firing ceased, and the delegates sent by the Governor of Astorga to treat about the capitulation of the garrison were received in the trenches by the Duke of Abrantes, who required, as a preliminary article, that the French troops should get possession of the great gate on the Valladolid road. General Thomier, accompanied by one of the Spanish delegates, ordered Captain Ware and me to follow him with our companies through the trenches to the gate above mentioned, and when he saw us properly installed there, and our sentinels placed inside the gate, he retired.

Scarcely had he gone away, when Colonel Coutard, of the 65th regiment, came to claim the right of having the gate occupied by his soldiers, as it was his regiment which attacked the town on that side the day before, etc. He ordered Captain Ware to remove his sentinels and to have his placed in their stead.

Ware refused, saying he was on guard, and that he would only execute the orders of General Thomier, who placed him there, or those of the generals higher in command, as General Solignac, or Junot, general-in-chief, etc. "I should refuse my own colonel if he were to give me orders, circumstanced as I am; then I trust, colonel, you cannot expect I will execute yours."

Some other words ensued between them, when Colonel Coutard said, "I must put you under arrest."

Captain Ware replied, "Colonel, I shall keep my arrest when I am off guard, but not till then!"

We regretted having had anything disagreeable with the colonel of the 65th, knowing as we did from an officer in his regiment, our countryman, Captain O'Kean, that he had the greatest respect for the Irish in the French service. He obtained the cross of the Legion of Honour for several of his officers after their brilliant defence of Ratisbon in 1809. Captain O'Kean was one of the first he proposed as having well merited to be a knight of the Legion of Honour: a distinction at that period not granted except for real service. Our altercation with Colonel Coutard soon finished. The Spanish garrison surrendered at discretion, and the Irish regiment was ordered to assemble and draw up in a line on the glacis of the town, to receive the prisoners and to escort them to Valladolid.

Five thousand brave Spanish soldiers marched out with all the honours of war, and laid down their arms on the glacis, in presence of the 8th corps of the French Army. Those prisoners had the satisfaction to witness a specimen of French discipline ere they marched away. The battalion of French troops that entered with the Spanish civil authorities to keep order and to furnish patrols and rounds through the town, arrested a man who contrived to get in before them and was plundering a house; he was brought out to the glacis, and, by order of the Duke of Abrantes, shot forthwith, as a warning to those ambulant speculators and followers of armies, who never have anything to sell but trumpery of the worst sort, their object being to get wealth by other means.

It was consolatory to see the horrors of war mitigated by a brave and humane chief; and indeed, on this occasion the Duke of Abrantes was entitled to the greatest praise; he required that the troops lodged in the place should observe the same order and discipline which they would have been forced to maintain in a town in the interior of France. What a striking contrast compared to the conduct of the English at Bada-joz in 1812, where Wellington allowed his army, during twenty-four hours, to commit all kinds of horrors on the innocent inhabitants, his allies, after the French garrison had capitulated and were marched off prisoners of war! and again at Saint-Sebastien the crimes perpetrated there make one shudder to hear them described. Though, indeed, I should not have been surprised at the want of English discipline from the knowledge I have had of the cruelties committed by the regiment of Ancient Britons in my own unfortunate country, Ireland, in 1798.

The 47th and 70th regiments of the line, known (until 1792) as Walsh's and Berwick's Irish brigades, made part of our army before Astorga; many of the officers of those regiments were Irishmen, some born in France, and others in Ireland. I was very intimate with two of them, O'Neill of the 47th, and Brennan of the 70th. Those of-ficers had often heard of the Irish patriots of '98, fighting, not for a pretender, but for the independence of their beloved country. Well, they had at Astorga the satisfaction of seeing some of those patriots of '98 distinguish themselves so as to be the admiration of the army, and Captain Brennan told me, that such was the enthusiasm about the bravery of the Irish, that his regiment would boast of having sprung from Berwick's.

Here is an honourable trait of an Irish officer in the Spanish ser-vice.

On our march from Astorga to Toro, I got, in the morning before we came to that town, charge of several Spanish officers, prisoners of war, who were on their way to France. General Thomier, in giving me the command of the escort, prayed me, as the march would be rather long, to render it as agreeable as possible to those officers, and at the same time he presented one of them to me, a Major Dorran, whose uncle I knew in Dublin, living in Francis Street. Mr. Dorran told me that his comrades in misfortune were military men of distinction, and that they were glad to be escorted by his countrymen.

After we had breakfasted at the half-way halt, I found Major Dor-ran a little indisposed. I wanted him to mount my horse, but he pre-ferred, if I would allow him, to get up on one of the baggage waggons. I gave him in charge to the sergeant who had care of our luggage. The rear guard and baggage arrived in due time at Toro; Major Dorran was not with them, and the poor sergeant could give me no account of how he escaped. This was a very unpleasant circumstance for me to have to report to the general in the morning. However, just as I was preparing to go to bed, about eleven o'clock at night, Major Dorran came to my room; he wanted to apologise for having remained behind. Seeing he was distressed lest I should think badly of him, I said: "Major, you were not on *parole*, you had not pledged your word of honour."

"No," he replied, "but could anything be more dishonourable than to have availed myself, of my countryman's kindness to me to escape, and to have him censured and injured on my account? Oh, no!" he repeated, "a thousand deaths before dishonour."

The feelings of this brave man must have been painful indeed, separated from his wife and two young children, whom he left in Galicia, near Corunna, in the care of her family. I had a bed prepared for him, and in the morning, I conducted him to rejoin his comrades, who had spent the night in prison, and they were marched off under a French officer's command. We heard some days after that two of these prisoners effected their escape on the road to Burgos, and that Major Dorran was one of them.

The day our vanguard, commanded by General Sainte-Croix, attacked the English General Stewart's advanced posts, and beat them back under the walls of the Fort of Conception and Almeida, whilst we were waiting to let our men repose themselves, General Sainte-Croix came and sat down amongst us, and began to praise our men, when Commandant Ware said: "General, they are not contented with you."

"What, then, have I done to displease them?" replied the general.

"Well, they say that in every instance where they expected to charge the enemy with their bayonets, you got before them with your cavalry, and left them very little share of the victory."

We all joined Commandant Ware, and repeated that it was but too true.

"Oh! gentlemen, you have a peculiar way of paying compliments." He then shook hands with us.

Two months after, when we were marching along the Tagus, down to Santarem, we were shocked indeed to see General Sainte-Croix killed by a cannon ball from one of the enemy's gunboats on the river. He was a splendid officer of cavalry, and he had done much to retrieve the reputation of the dragoons in Spain. Napoleon had the highest opinion of his talents and worth, and would have made him one of the marshals of France had he lived. I never heard of a general so universally regretted as he was, so amiable and so brave, that it was a pleasure to speak to him.

Although the 70th regiment, in which Captain William Corbet was, belonged to our army, and had made the campaigns in Spain and Portugal with us, I had never met him after he left the Irish legion at Alençon in 1806, though I frequently heard about him from some of his comrades. Captain Brennan, who was badly wounded beside Captain Corbet on the 3rd of April, stopped a day and a night at Ciudad Rodrigo, where we were in garrison. He told me that their *chef de bataillon* and their colonel were both killed, and that Captain Corbet, as senior officer, took the command of the battalion, and showed the greatest coolness and bravery during the action.

On the 3rd of May, 1811, when Marshal Massena's army was arriving in the plain before the town of Rodrigo, taking a walk through the camp, I came to the bivouac of the 70th regiment, when I saw Captain Corbet very busy endeavouring to get something cooked for his dinner. He had a very poor supply of provisions, and as he could not come into town with me, I brought one of his men, and sent him out all I could procure: a loaf of white bread and a few bottles of wine. Though we had many things to say to one another, after a lapse of five years that we had not met, that pleasure was deferred to a more favourable occasion, I being in a hurry to return to town. We, however, met frequently afterwards when he was on Marshal Marmont's staff. I must say that Captain Corbet in his new situation was always obliging and friendly to his former comrades, of which I shall speak in the next chapter.

The departure of H.R.H. the Prince Regent of Portugal for the Brazils

CHAPTER 6

Operations in Portugal

The reorganisation of the Army of Portugal into six divisions under the command of Marshal Marmont, on account of the reduced
state of the 2nd, 6th and 8th corps of which it was composed, was
considered a wise measure; and the young generals put at the head of
the divisions, such as Foy, Brenier, Mauguin, etc., and Marshal Clauzel,
then general of division commandant, created great emulation in the
army; besides, the marshal himself at that time had acquired a high
reputation as general-in-chief, and his staff was composed of several
distinguished officers. General Fabvier, of such notoriety in Greece,
was then a captain, as was Count Denys de Damremont, afterward the
general-in-chief who was killed in Africa at the siege of Constantine.
General Corbet was another of the staff captains, and from the experience he had acquired as an infantry officer of the 70th regiment of the
line, and his perfect knowledge of the French and English languages
(writing both equally well), he rendered much service, and he was
greatly esteemed by the Duke of Ragusa, Marshal Marmont.

Our general of division was the brave Brenier who made the sur-
prising march through the English Army after he had blown up the
ramparts of Almeida. The Irish officers were delighted to be in his division; but they regretted not to be still in General Thomier's brigade,
who befriended them on all occasions, and who was so much liked by
all the soldiers of the regiment. During the retreat out of Portugal he
shared in all their dangers and miseries, and constantly bivouacked at
the head of the Irish battalion.

One instance will show why the soldiers took him into their consideration. When the army fell back from the line of Torres Vedras,
the Irish battalion stopped with General Thomier in the village of
Prosseras. He ordered one day that I should make a reconnaissance
with my grenadiers on the enemy's line, to return when I perceived

93

them, and to bring the cattle I met on the way, and provisions of any kind.

When I returned I had to report him that during my expedition I never saw a human being or living animal of any sort; that I had discovered a quantity of tanned leather in one place, hidden in the mountains; in another a room filled with white wax for making candles; that two of my grenadiers were missing, and that I feared they had been taken prisoners. He invited me to dinner, and just as we were going to sit down to table, at half-past six o'clock in the evening, my sergeant-major came to tell me that the two grenadiers who had remained behind had arrived with two head of horn cattle.

General Thomier exclaimed: "Send them here forthwith, they must dine with us." And he ordered his servant to prepare places for them at the table. He was enchanted with these brave men. They told him how they had contrived to procure the cattle; they said they had "extracted" them from the English cattle grazing in fields at a great distance. The expression made all the company laugh, and the general had a bumper filled to drink to their health.

Whenever we were marching near where General Thomier's division was stopping, in the summer and autumn of 1811, I availed myself of the occasion to go and visit him, and have some conversation with him respecting our not being yet known to our new generals, etc. "Never mind," he would reply. "You will be soon advantageously known to them." A few days after, he gave me a certificate of my services to present to these generals if I chose to do so. Although I did not want to make use of that certificate at the time, it was consoling to me to have a testimonial from a general of worth and of high reputation, in whose brigade the Irish regiment was so actively employed at the sieges of Astorga, Ciudad Rodrigo and Almeida, and in the campaigns of Portugal.

Besides, I was in very low spirits on account of Commandant Fitzhenry's sad affair, and from being separated from some of my best friends and comrades Captain Allen a prisoner of war, Commandant Ware gone to Landau, and Captain Murray, from ill health, obliged to return to France. Although Captains O'Malley and Brangan, who were equally my friends, were remaining, and braver or more honourable men could not be, still they did not possess the resources necessary to take advantage and get the situation left vacant of *chef de bataillon*. They were senior to me, and I feared that place would be filled by some *protégé* sent from Paris, who had no claims on the Irish regiment.

General Brenier's division marched back to Salamanca and the neighbourhood of Toro; but on the 1st of June, 1811, the army was united and reviewed by Marshal Marmont, and on the 4th marched from Salamanca and went through the province of Estramadura, passing by Banos and Placentia, crossing the Tagus at Lugar Nueva on a bridge of boats brought there by the army, to Truxillo, Merida, and to Badajos, to attack the English and Portuguese Army, then laying siege to that town. By the time the French Army arrived there, they had already made two breaches, and only for this rapid march of the French Army of Portugal, combined with that of Marshal Soult from Seville, Badajos would have been taken by the English and Portuguese and Spaniards, who were thus obliged to retire behind Elvas into Portugal. This was from the 17th to the 20th of June, 1811.

After sending provisions of every kind for six months into Badajos, for the garrison, and getting the breaches repaired, the army retired into different cantonments in Estramadura. The Irish battalion remained some time at Truxillo, and from thence marched to Avilar, passing by Naval Maral, the headquarters of Marshal Marmont. They had pleasant quarters in the mountains during the hot summer of the comet of 1811, the soldiers being well fed and well lodged for the months of July and August.

In the beginning of September, the captain of grenadiers, Byrne, (the author), of the Irish battalion was ordered with his company and the company of *voltigeurs* of the Irish regiment to General Brenier's headquarters at Bexar. On the 19th the army marched to form a junction with the army corps of the north, commanded by General Count Dorsenne, for the purpose of relieving Rodrigo, at that time besieged and blockaded by the English, and of throwing provisions into it. The two French Armies met on the 24th, and on the 25th marched on Rodrigo. During this expedition the Irish companies, commanded by the captain of grenadiers, Byrne, were in the advance guard, and took part in the different actions that took place in raising the siege, and in driving the English and Portuguese into Portugal on the 27th, 28th and 29th of September, at Fontelgenalgo and Alfitas.

The Irish companies *d'élite* returned back to Rodrigo on the 1st of October, and from thence marched with General Brenier to Placentia, his headquarters. They were there united with the centre companies to do garrison duty, and with another of the 65th. General Dejean, who had just got his brevet, got the command of the brigade, and replaced General Godar.

On the 13th of October, 1811, the captain of grenadiers, Byrne, of the Irish battalion having his company, with the company of *voltigeurs* of the same regiment assembled to pass an inspection, heard the *générale* beat, and was apprised that the enemy's cavalry, to the number of fifteen hundred, was drawn up in line within gunshot of the town; he immediately marched to attack them with his two companies formed in column by section ready to form a hollow square, and he succeeded in dispersing and driving them a great distance off before the rest of the troops of the garrison had time to be assembled.

General Brenier soon joined him with his *aides-de-camp* and staff officers, all mounted, and when night came on, and the enemy had effected their retreat, he was so delighted with the conduct of the soldiers, that he gave them all the money he had on him to drink when they returned to Placentia; and the morning after, he gave the following order of the division:

Placentia, le 14 Octobre, 1811.
Ordre du Jour de la Division.

Hier, lors de l'appel aux armes des compagnies d'élite de la garnison, Monsieur le générale de division a remarqué que celles du bataillon Irlandais se sont distinguées particuliérement par leur bravoure, leur zéle et leur exactitude à se rendre au point indiqué. Il leur en témoigne sa satisfaction.

  Signé:

Le générale de division,
Brenier.

Translation of the foregoing Order of the Day:—

Placentia, 14th October, 1811.
Order of the Day of the Division.

Yesterday, when the call to arms was made of the companies *d'élite* of the garrison, the general of division observed that those of the Irish battalion particularly distinguished themselves by their bravery and zeal, and by their promptitude and exactness in repairing to the point they were ordered to. He testifies to them his satisfaction at their conduct.

  Signed:

The General of Division,
Brenier.

It was whilst the battalion stopped at Placentia that the first news of Captain Allen being a prisoner of war in a fort near Cadiz was received. After the exertions that had been made to have him exchanged in the month of April at Rodrigo failed, as will be seen in the following note made at the time, it was agreeable to know that he was not given up to the English then at Cadiz. As soon as the prisoners were escorted to Rodrigo, Captain Byrne waited on the governor, General Rheno, to pray him to keep one of the officers, a nephew to Don Julian, the chief of the guerrilla band which took Captain Allen prisoner, in order to have them exchanged.

The general not only consented, but took the most lively interest in having the exchange carried into effect immediately, when he learned from Captain Byrne the cruel fate that awaited poor Allen if he were handed over to the English general. (It was feared he might be executed as a rebel. S. G.) He forthwith got the Spanish *prefet* to procure a confidential person to carry a letter from the Spanish officer to his uncle Don Julian, supplicating him to give up Captain Allen, and saying that another officer and himself would be exchanged for him. The messenger returned, after four days' absence, with an answer that Captain Allen had been sent to a depot of prisoners of war, without mentioning the name of the place. In consequence the Spanish officer was sent off to join the other prisoners at Salamanca on their way to France, and Allen's comrades were left to conjecture whether or not he was still in existence.

This took place about the end of April, 1811, and until the end of September the same year there was no news whatever of Captain Allen, when Captain Byrne, being at Placentia, received a letter from him, dated the prison of Cadiz, and containing all the details of what he had suffered, the manner he had been taken prisoner, etc., etc.

The same day Captain Byrne enclosed to General Séméle, chief of the staff to Marshal Victor, then commanding the French Army before Cadiz, a French treasury bill of a thousand *francs*, which he fortunately happened to have at the time; he begged the general to have it changed into Spanish money and to have it forwarded to Captain Allen in his prison; he also prayed him to have the goodness to use his influence to have Captain Allen exchanged, lest he should be given up to the English.

Captain Byrne wrote immediately to Major Lawless at Bois-le-Duc, where he had then the command of the Irish regiment, and enclosed him a copy of Captain Allen's letter, requesting him also to use his influence with the Minister of War to have Captain Allen exchanged before he could fall into the hands of the English.

When Captain Byrne returned in October, 1811, to Placentia, after the expedition to relieve Rodrigo terminated, he waited on Marshal Marmont about Captain Allen's unfortunate situation, gave him a detailed *Memoir* on the subject, which the marshal approved and promised to have it forwarded immediately to Marshal Victor, who commanded before Cadiz, and he added that he would use his own influence, and when any prisoners were made, he should propose an exchange for Captain Allen. Captain Byrne availed himself of being at headquarters to endeavour to get Allen exchanged, and neglected no opportunity that could tend to that end: indeed, he could not have acted otherwise, for they were always on the most friendly terms, and were the best comrades. Captain Allen's purse was ever at his disposition, therefore Captain Byrne felt the greatest happiness to have had the thousand *francs* to send to Captain Allen.

That sum was paid to Captain Byrne on the 30th of December, 1811, at Talavera de la Reyna by Giraud, the officer paymaster to the 2nd battalion, when all arrears due to the officers were paid up in full, previous to their returning to France; and the appointments and arrears due to Captain Allen were received up to the 26th of March, 1811, the day he was made a prisoner, and deposited in the military chest of the battalion, which was brought to the depot at Bois-le-Duc in Holland, and there given up to Colonel Lawless and the council of administration of the Irish regiment. When Captain Allen arrived at Bois-le-Duc in 1812, after he had the good fortune to be exchanged, he found all his accounts and affairs properly settled to his liking by the quartermaster of the regiment.

Captain Dillon, who had been one of the *aides-de-camp* to the Duke of Abrantes, got his brevet of *chef de bataillon* to the 2nd battalion of the Irish regiment, and joined it at Placentia in November, 1811.

In the beginning of December, 1811, Marshal Marmont ordered a court-martial to be assembled to try Commandant Fitzhenry by contumacy, accused of desertion to the enemy. It was presided by the colonel of the 17th Leger regiment, and composed six other officers, from the 22nd and 65th regiments of the line. It met in a village where the colonel of the 17th commanded, four leagues from Placentia. After hearing all the evidence that had been procured from the 22nd of April, 1811, the day on which he was taken prisoner, down to the assembling of the court-martial, four of the members of the court declared that he was guilty, three that he was not. As it is necessary according to the French military code to have five out of the seven members forming a court-martial to condemn, Fitzhenry was acquitted.

On the 6th of December, 1811, the Irish battalion was ordered to Casa de Cadas, and from thence to Montbeltran, in the mountains, to relieve the 28th regiment, which had been there some time. Lieutenant Malony, with 50 men of the Irish battalion, was ordered to go to a town eight leagues from Montbeltran to escort back a convoy of mules loaded with provisions. After he had passed a mountain four leagues off, he met a French battalion that had been harassed and attacked by the guerrillas in the plain through which Malony had to pass.

The chief of the French battalion wanted Malony to return with him, saying he surely could not think of advancing with so small a detachment against five hundred men, all well mounted; but Malony, having a written order, thought he could not with honour return before he met the enemy, and was forced to retreat. He accordingly proceeded, and, as the chief of the battalion led him to expect, soon met the enemy, and was obliged to take a position amongst the rocks, on the side of a hill, to defend himself. The guerrillas finding they could not bring Malony and his men down into the plain, and night coming on, filed off to a small village just by.

Lieutenant Malony on this left his position and pursued them into the village, where they were scattered in disorder; he beat them out of it, barricaded all the outlets, and defended himself all night and until eight o'clock the next morning, when fortunately, he was relieved by a regiment that had marched several leagues, having heard the day before of the fighting. Malony then continued his march and escorted back to Montbeltran his convoy with great *éclat*. This was not the only time he distinguished himself in the like manner.

As soon as he returned to France, Colonel Lawless obtained for him his brevet of captain in the 2nd battalion of the Irish regiment. He was one of those unfortunate Irishmen given up to the King of Prussia by the English Government. He had been wounded and taken prisoner in Ireland after General Humbert surrendered, and was in the Prussian Army and taken a prisoner by the French at the Battle of Iena, after which he entered the Irish regiment in the service of France, along with those other Irishmen who had been taken prisoners at Iena, and who had been given up in a like manner to the Prussian Government by England.

During the month of December, 1811, Marshal Marmont ordered

the different divisions of his army to manoeuvre and change cantonments. The 6th division commanded by General Brenier was on march, when at Naval Maral he received orders for all the officers, noncommissioned officers, corporals and drummers of the 2nd Irish battalion to go into France, and to leave behind them all the private soldiers, to be incorporated into the Prussian regiment in the French service, and then in garrison at Lugar Nueva and Almiras on the Tagus.

On the 25th of December, 1811, General Brenier, accompanied by the military inspector, performed this very painful duty of separating the men from their officers, under whose orders they had been serving for four years in Spain, and to whom they were much attached. The general declared he never before witnessed so distressing a scene as three or four hundred men in the greatest grief and weeping at taking leave of their officers; he added he thought it cruel and impolitic thus to separate them.

The officers, non-commissioned officers, corporals and drummers, in all about 120, marched for France, and arrived at Talavera de la Reyna on the 27th of December. They stopped there three days to receive all arrears, then set out again and arrived at Toledo on the 1st of January, 1812. From thence they proceeded to Madrid, where they had to wait ten days, being too few in number to march without a large convoy of troops.

A rather unpleasant incident took place at the gates of Madrid in January, 1812, between the sons of two distinguished Irishmen. One was the son of the unfortunate Theobald Dillon, general of division, who was murdered by his own soldiers in the Revolution, near Lille. The other was the son of General O'Neill, who was colonel of Walsh's regiment in 1792, when it took the number of 47 of the French line. These sons of theirs were captains in the Army of Portugal; they had recently been promoted to the superior rank of *chef de bataillon*: O'Neill to the 47th regiment, and Dillon to the command of the 2nd battalion of the Irish regiment.

The latter, marching out of Madrid at the head of the *cadre* of that battalion, was accosted by Commandant O'Neill, who said to him, "Commandant Dillon, you cannot proceed far, as my company of *voltigeurs* is placed at half a league on the high road to prevent any one passing until the column of troops forming the convoy is organised by the general, and my battalion is ordered to be the vanguard."

"Very well," said Commandant Dillon, still continuing to march till he was stopped by the captain of the *voltigeurs* of the 47th, to whom he showed his order to return to France.

The captain very properly replied, "Such orders, *commandant*, do not regard me, mine are to let no one pass here till the column is put on march by the general's order, and I am determined to execute my *consigne, quoi qu'il en coûte*." Commandant Dillon being on horseback, and about twenty yards ahead, seeing his small column stopped by the men of the 47th, ordered it to advance, and the captain of grenadiers of the Irish had the disagreeable task of pushing the *voltigeurs* of the 47th aside, to open a passage to march forward, and obey an unwise chief.

Notwithstanding the dangerous state of the country, he had to march through, owing to the guerrillas being every day in sight, Commandant Dillon made his way to Valladolid with his 120 men, but in this town, he had to wait eighteen days.

It was on this march from Madrid that, passing by the town of Segovia, Lieutenant Jackson seized the occasion to show off his wit and turn for bantering. Seeing a group of Spaniards, with their brown cloaks thrown over their shoulders, examining and counting the troops that halted on the place, as was their custom on such occasions, he addressed these solemn gentlemen, saying, pointing to the tower, that he wished to know if it was there that Gil Blas was imprisoned. They replied, it was the town prison. He then very politely begged one of them to accompany him, that he wished to ascertain the precise room which had been occupied by that truly enlightened Spaniard during his confinement in the tower.

"Oh! *señor*," one said, "*Gil Blas* is a mere romance;" to which Jackson replied, he was sorry to find they did not know the history of their country better: that it was a true narrative, and that only for the Inquisition, Le Sage would have published it in quite a different form and given the real names of the persons alluded to. One of the Spanish gentlemen, seeing Jackson so serious and bent upon visiting the tower, accompanied him through every part of it, whilst Jackson made notes, and he fain would have persuaded his comrades that the Spaniards were delighted with the information he gave them.

This was only one of many instances when Jackson by his humour and gaiety made his comrades often forget their miseries and privations. One morning, at the bivouac of the Irish regiment at the lines of Torres Vedras, whilst waiting for orders, the officers stood chatting together, when General Thomier beckoned one of them to come to him and tell him what the very animated conversation was about which he observed going on. He was told that it was Lieutenant Jackson holding forth and maintaining that there could be no comparison between roast mutton and roast beef, provided the latter was "underdone" *à l'anglaise*. "Oh! *par exemple, c'est un peu trop fort.*"

"What," he asked, "did Captain O'Malley say on the matter?"

"Oh, that it was cruel and inhuman to talk of roast meat of any kind to men who were starving, and when none could be had for love or money."

"Captain O'Malley is right," said the general. Jackson bore up against adversity in the same gay manner. Captain Hutteau, the Mayor of Malesherbes, who was a prisoner of war in Russia along with Jackson, (captured in the action at Goldberg, in Silesia, August, 1813), takes infinite pleasure in talking to us about Jackson and his courage and vivacity in very trying circumstances. Monsieur de Buisson also, a French magistrate, has given some excellent articles to the *Siècle* newspaper on his sufferings whilst a prisoner of war in Russia, when a *sous*-lieutenant of only nineteen years of age. He speaks of Captain Jackson in every trial and hardship they had to undergo with the greatest admiration and gratitude till they were exchanged in 1814.

During this time, January, 1812, Ciudad Rodrigo was taken by the English before Marshal Marmont had time to arrive with his army to relieve it.

Two splendid standards in green, on which was written in gold letters: "Independence of Ireland," and which were sent to the 2nd and 3rd Irish battalions by order of the emperor, and which had been at Valladolid from the year before, were brought back to the depot by the officers of the 2nd battalion, who, after a long and fatiguing march, arrived on the 11th of April, 1812, at Bois-le-Duc in Holland, then the depot of the Irish regiment instead of Landau.

At the end of February, 1812, Lieutenant-Colonel Lawless got his brevet of colonel, and the command of the regiment, which, by a decree of the emperor, was now called, "*Troisième régiment étranger, Irlandais*." By the same decree, the other foreign regiments were numbered:

That of Latour-d'Auvergne, No. 1;

That of Isenberg, No. 2;

The Irish, No. 3;

The Prussian regiment, No. 4.

Commandant Mahony, at the same time, was named *gros-major*, or lieutenant-colonel to the Irish regiment. Commandant Tennant was with the 1st battalion of the Irish regiment in the island of Goree, in Holland; Commandant Ware with the 3rd battalion at Williamstadt on the Meuse. The 4th battalion and depot received nearly fifteen hundred Germans and other foreigners who had been in the Dutch Army, but who, in consequence of Holland becoming a part of France, were sent to the foreign regiments in the French service. Eight hundred of these brave men were drafted into the 2nd battalion, just arrived from Spain, which completed it, and on the 18th of April it marched to Bergen-op-Zoom, to form the garrison there, and to prepare for joining the Grand Army.

Captain Hayne, who had served in the 20th regiment of the line in Italy, got his brevet as *commandant* of the 4th battalion, and joined it at Bois-le-Duc in 1812.

Captain Allen, who had been detained a prisoner at Cadiz, had the good fortune to be exchanged, and arrived at the depot of the regiment at Bois-le-Duc at the end of the year 1812. But there was no chance then of his obtaining the advancement he so well merited by his brilliant conduct at Astorga in Spain. All vacancies that had occurred in the regiment for superior officers were filled up, and many of them by those who, having been born in France, were entitled to advancement in French regiments; which was not just to the Irish officers, whose promotion was confined to their own regiment. Colonel Lawless, however, promised Captain Allen that, in the event of the regiment going into campaign, he should have the command of his company of *voltigeurs* in the 2nd battalion.

The Duke of Feltre, on the recommendation of Colonel Lawless, recompensed many of the subaltern officers coming out of Spain. Lieutenants Malony, Delany, Bowling, Burke and Jackson received their brevets of captains; and Ensigns MacEgan, Brelevet, etc., theirs of lieutenants. Many non-commissioned officers were also promoted to the rank of ensign.

Ensign Keller, who was taken prisoner in Portugal by the English, escaped from England and joined the depot at Bois-le-Duc. Ensign Ryan, who was taken prisoner at Flushing in August, 1809, also escaped from prison and joined the regiment in 1812. Colonel Lawless obtained advancement for both these officers, and they got their brevets as lieutenants, and were placed in the war battalions.

Colonel Lawless obtained promotion for all the officers of the 2nd battalion that were called into France from Spain in 1812, except Captains O'Malley and Byrne, and the recompense these two officers considered themselves entitled to after the four or five severe campaigns they had just made was the decoration of the Legion of Honour. On their way through Paris in March, 1812, they waited on the Minister of War, and presented him a demand, backed by several of the generals under whose orders they had been serving. His reception was most favourable: so much so, that they left Paris for the depot in the highest spirits. The minister wrote to Colonel Lawless to know about their merits, conduct, etc.; and whether it was that the demand had not been forwarded by him to the minister as chief of the corps, or that he wished to see his superior officers decorated before the captains.

It is probable, nay even certain, that he gave the last reason to the minister, for he could not have given any other; as neither of these captains had ever been under his orders, he could not well judge of their merits to obtain the knighthood in the Legion of Honour. But let that be as it may, it was very unfortunate that poor Captain O'Malley did not obtain it at that epoch, for shortly after he became stone blind, and had to retire on a small pension with a wife and two children; 250 *francs* a year was thus lost for the last thirty-two years to as brave a man as ever left Ireland.

As to Captain Byrne, he had only to wait to make another campaign, the year after, when he got it; but it is not less true that he felt much disappointed and very sore on the subject, particularly so on account of being on such friendly terms with Colonel Lawless from the first moment he became acquainted with him; and indeed again, at Bergen-op-Zoom, in January, 1813, previous to leaving that town to join the Grand Army, he had to complain of the want of decision in his favour on the part of Colonel Lawless, who was on the point of giving his company of grenadiers to Captain O'Reilly, who claimed it as his right, he having commanded, he said, a grenadiers company longer than Captain Byrne, though the latter was his senior as a captain for more than a year.

The 3rd battalion, to which O'Reilly belonged, remaining in Holland, he very naturally wished to get into one of the war battalions going into campaign. Colonel Lawless submitted Captain O'Reilly's claim to the Minister of War, who decided against him and in favour of Captain Byrne; but this decision of the minister only arrived when the regiment was in presence of the enemy on the Elbe, and kept Captain Byrne in a disagreeable state of suspense whilst waiting for the decision.

At the end of this memorable campaign of 1813, and the beginning of the next, 1814, Captain Byrne being actively employed in Holland and at Antwerp, commanding a battalion at the advanced posts before the enemy, was quite sure of obtaining his brevet of *chef de bataillon*, as he was proposed on the field of battle at Goldberg the 24th of August, 1813, with three other captains, by General Puthod, and the demand was backed by General Lauriston, commander of the 5th corps of the army.

There seemed no doubt of these commissions being granted, but still Captain Byrne was doomed to be disappointed, for as soon as the communication was opened after the siege of Antwerp, the colonel of the regiment, Mahony, received intelligence that Captains Allen and O'Reilly were promoted, and that Captains Byrne and Saint-Leger might expect their brevets also; but from the change of government, and the vast number of claimants, he entertained little hopes.

Captain Byrne seeing two Prussian captains in the French service of the name of Geitz getting their commissions as chiefs of battalion, in the month of October, asked leave of absence for three months, and came to Paris in December, 1814. He saw Marshal Soult (Minister of War) twice in February, 1815, who received him very well, and promised him the first place vacant in any of the three foreign regiments as chief of battalion; but he left the ministry, and the Hundred Days came on before Captain Byrne could get his brevet.

It is only justice to the memory of General Lawless to say he did everything at this time to assist Captain Byrne to obtain his commission, but unfortunately it was too late, and Captain Byrne had in consequence to live on the miserable half pay as a captain for more than twelve years, until his ever-to-be-lamented friend, Colonel O'Neill, chief of the personnel of the War Office, got him employed in 1828 on the staff of General Maison on the expedition to Greece; and on the 4th of September, 1830, being in Greece, he received his brevet as chief of the 2nd battalion of the 56th regiment of the line, then at Grenoble, commanded by Colonel Bugeaud, afterwards Marshal of France.

Colonel Lawless showed the greatest activity and talent for the administration as well as the instruction and discipline of his regiment. He passed the summer months of 1812 visiting and inspecting the different battalions detached in Holland, and holding them ready to march at a moment's notice.

CHAPTER 7

Operations Along the Elbe

As soon as the 29th bulletin of the Grand Army, dated November, 1812, appeared in the newspapers, with the account of the disasters of the retreat from Moscow, Colonel Lawless wrote to the Minister of War, the Duke of Feltre, in the name of all the officers of the regiment, soliciting in the most earnest terms to be employed in the Grand Army. The minister answered Colonel Lawless immediately in the most friendly manner and acceded to his demand; he ordered him to complete the 1st and 2nd battalions to a thousand each, and to make every necessary preparation for the ensuing campaign.

By the month of January, 1813, all was ready. On the 30th of January, orders arrived for the regiment to march to Magdeburg, and on the 1st of February, Commandant Tennant, with the 1st battalion, then in the island of Goree, set out, going through Holland to Osnaburg.

The 2nd battalion, under Commandant Ware, began to march also on the 1st of February for Magdeburg, quitting Bergen-op-Zoom and going by Breda, Tilbury, Bois-le-Duc, crossing the Meuse at Grave, the Waal at Nimeguen, and the Rhine at Wesel, to Münster, and then to Osnaburg, where it arrived the same day as the 1st battalion.

This was the first time these two battalions had been together since they separated at Flushing in 1808, the 2nd battalion having been more than four years in Spain. The meeting of the officers of the two battalions which belonged to the former Irish legion, after so long a separation, was very agreeable to them all.

Colonel Lawless, after inspecting the two united battalions, marched at the head of his regiment by Minden, where they crossed the Weser, to Hanover, Brunswick, etc., to Magdeburg, where they arrived on the 28th of February, and though in the depth of winter, had but few men in the hospitals, and left none behind, for which the colonel and officers were highly complimented by General Lauriston when he passed the review of the regiment on the 1st of March, 1813, at Magdeburg. He was delighted to see two thousand men so well equipped and having a splendid band of music, and everything else in style and order.

Colonel William O'Mara, who had been a captain in the Irish legion at its formation in 1803, was now Commandant Superior of Magdeburg; he had been first *aide-de-camp* to Marshal Lannes, and was wounded the day the marshal was killed at the Battle of Wagram in 1809; he was twin brother to Daniel O'Mara who commanded the Irish regiment for a short time in Spain, and their elder brother, General O'Mara, had the honour of commanding the town of Dunkirk, and seeing the English Army under the Duke of York forced to abandon the siege and fly in disorder before the French citizens armed for its defence and their liberty.

The town of Magdeburg was at this time crowded beyond measure with the cohorts of the first band of the National Guards arriving there to be organised into regiments of the line, and to be comprised in the new corps about to be formed. General Lauriston was named commander-in-chief of the 5th corps, to be composed of four divisions. The 1st division was commanded by General Maison, the 2nd by General Puthod, the 3rd by General Lagrange, the 4th by General Rochambeau. The Irish regiment was to make part of the 3rd division of the 5th corps; but none of these divisions were yet assembled and there were no troops, or scarcely any, to guard the line of the Elbe from Magdeburg to Hamburg; the army which retreated with the viceroy, Eugène Beauharnais, being employed from Magdeburg to Dresden.

On the 3rd of March, 1813, the Irish regiments left Magdeburg and marched to Stendal, and from this town detached several companies along the Elbe to guard the passages, and then proceeded to Arandsee, Seehausen, etc. The enemy by this time had an army corps on the other side of the Elbe near Werben. Colonel Lawless got orders to call in all his detachments and to fall back on Stendal, where the regiment was again united on the 17th of March. The general of brigade, General Montbrun (brother to the lieutenant-general of the same name), had a brigade of cavalry at Stendal; he gave orders for all the baggage to be sent off to Magdeburg, and even thought that he had not force enough to resist the enemy that had already passed the river.

On the 18th and 19th their advanced posts approached Stendal; on the 20th, General Montbrun decided to attack them. He gave the command of the infantry, consisting of two regiments, to Colonel Lawless, who ordered the two companies of *voltigeurs* commanded by Captains Allen and O'Reilly to flank the column, and the two companies of grenadiers, commanded by Captains Byrne and MacCarthy, to make the vanguard and to begin the attack.

The enemy was beaten back to Werben and driven through the town in great disorder, as the grenadiers, with the French cavalry, entered pell-mell with them into the town. Several were lost repassing the river, and a number of horses abandoned; four officers and a great many private soldiers were taken prisoners. Notwithstanding this brilliant success, General Montbrun thought it prudent to return in the night to Stendal, and, on the second day after the regiment marched, returned again with General Russel by Werben.

Commandant Tennant's battalion made a reconnaissance on the road to Seehausen, and met the enemy in force. The Prince of Eckmühl, Marshal Davoust, arrived and took the command. The Irish regiment, with the cavalry, made the vanguard of this army. On the 24th he attacked and beat the enemy from Seehausen. The adjutant-major, Captain Osmond, left the regiment to perform the functions of chief of the staff with General Montbrun, and did not again rejoin the regiment.

Whilst Commandant Ware and his battalion were at the *château* of Gartz and Schnakenburg, Captain Malony, who with his company had been the last on duty of the battalion, received orders to march; he flew into a violent passion and remonstrated with the adjutant-major, saying he would not march out of his turn; but when one of his comrades informed him he was chosen by the *commandant* on account of the importance and danger of the mission, which was to prevent the enemy passing the Elbe in the night, they having a large boat on the other side, a league down the river, Malony instantly exclaimed: "Ware was an excellent chief and showed his discernment and judgment in the orders he gave;" and repaired without delay to the place assigned, just in time to have his men concealed and to allow the enemy to approach in their boat within pistol shot, when he gave orders to fire on them.

This unexpected attack made them instantly return to the other side, and obliged them to abandon their plan for that night, thought they were in great force. Captain Malony had thus the honour of defending all the night this passage with his company alone.

The Irish regiment with the cavalry making the vanguard under

Marshal Davoust, after beating the enemy from Seehausen on the 24th of March, 1813, marched on the 26th to relieve General Morant, who was attacked by a superior force at Luneburg. They arrived in the night, after making a forced march of eighteen leagues, but unfortunately too late. The general had been already taken prisoner, and the enemy retreated across the Elbe with him and the other prisoners.

On the 28th of March, Commandant Ware was detached with his battalion to Winsen on the Elbe, and on the 29th, Colonel Lawless and the rest of the regiment marched to Salzwedel and joined General Puthod's division at a *château* that had belonged to the King of England. It bivouacked and remained several days near Salzwedel, and from thence went to Giffhorn in the beginning of April, at which place another bivouac was formed for a few days. Marshal Davoust lodged in an old castle, and had the grenadiers of the Irish regiment to guard him.

During his stay at this place, a young Russian officer was taken concealed in the village, who owned that he intended to carry the marshal away, if he could meet him walking out alone, as he was accustomed to do after dinner. The marshal showed, during the continual skirmishes he had with the enemy in this neighbourhood, the greatest activity, being always with the vanguard. When he was replaced by General Sebastiani, he spoke to him of the Irish regiment in the highest terms.

The enemy had taken possession of Uelzen, and were in great force, Russians and Prussians. General Sebastiani decided to attack them. He told the colonels and officers, when he received their visit, his intention to attack the enemy the next day; that they were ten thousand strong, that he had three thousand infantry and fifteen hundred cavalry, which he thought sufficient, and at the same time told Colonel Lawless he should have the honour of making the advance guard.

Accordingly, on the 22nd of April, at daylight, the enemy's posts were attacked and all driven back on Uelzen, which town they endeavoured to defend for a short time; but fearing their retreat might be cut off, they abandoned the place, no doubt with great reluctance, for, it being Easter Sunday (according to the old style observed by the Russians), they had all their preparations made for the feast they have on such occasions; and as they had observed Lent very strictly, it was a great disappointment to them to be forced to leave their fine repast, consisting of meat and other good things.

Colonel Lawless was appointed to command the place, and had

Commandant Tennant's battalion in the town to furnish the different guards, which was considered a great honour, as the rest of the army bivouacked outside the town. The greatest order was observed, and no inhabitant had the least complaint to make.

A spy, who had been detected two days before, was condemned by a court-martial in this town to be shot, but just as the *gendarmes* had placed him on his knees, and were about to fire, General Sebastiani ordered him to be saved. The unfortunate man ought to have been very grateful, for he had nothing to say in his defence.

After remaining two days at Uelzen, the army marched on Luneburg, where the enemy were again concentrating their forces, instead of re-crossing the Elbe. The Irish grenadiers, with the cavalry, made the vanguard, and when the enemy was beat, Colonel Lawless was ordered by General Sebastiani to take the command of the town, where, as at Uelzen, the best order was observed.

Commandant Ware, who had been detached with his battalion on the 28th of March to Winsen on the Elbe, was ordered to fall back on Celles, to join a French brigade, in which town he had a brilliant combat with the Cossacks. The town being evacuated by order one night, and the enemy allowed to take possession of it, in the morning they were attacked in the town and driven through it in great disorder. They set fire to a wooden bridge over the Aller, to cover their retreat, but Commandant Ware passed it on horseback through the flames with his battalion and beat them a great distance from the town, when he was ordered to return, and had scarcely time to repass the bridge before it was consumed.

It was on this occasion that General Aubert took a great liking to the Irish regiment. He was colonel of the 148th regiment, and was present when Ware passed the bridge; and when the general observed that Ware pursued the enemy too far, Colonel Aubert replied, "He would wish to be able to make the same reproach to his officers"— who were mostly Dutch, newly organised at Magdeburg.

On the 28th of April, 1813, Colonel Lawless heard at Luneburg of the emperor's arrival at the army; no news could have afforded more pleasure than this gave to the troops, as they all well knew that a general action would soon take place, which would put an end to the continual marching and counter-marching they had had during the months of March and April: for the enemy would, in the event of losing the battle, have to recross the Elbe immediately and concentrate their forces to make head against Napoleon and his Grand Army.

On the 1st of May, 1813, Colonel Lawless received orders to march to Brunswick with Commandant Tennant's battalion, to which town Commandant Ware had orders to repair from Celles with his battalion, and from thence the regiment was to proceed to Halberstadt, to wait for further orders from headquarters.

Nothing could be more flattering for the regiment than the praises the officers received from General Sebastiani, when they were presented to him by Colonel Lawless, previous to their departure for the Grand Army. He said that the good result of the different affairs on the Elbe, from the beginning of the campaign, was due to their activity and bravery. The colonel and corps of officers took leave also of General Puthod, as it was thought the regiment would join General Lagrange's division, to which it belonged, according to the organisation of the 5th corps.

On the 5th of May, 1813, the regiment was united at Brunswick, and from thence marched to Halberstadt. It arrived at this town on the 8th, where the news of the Battle of Lutzen was announced to the troops under arms. The joy they expressed was great indeed. Every soldier felt in this victory a recompense for all his fatigues.

Colonel Lawless, fearing that the orders for him might have been intercepted, detached an officer to General Lauriston with a letter and a report of everything concerning the regiment from the time it marched from Magdeburg, on the 3rd of March, down to the present day. He had to mention that the baggage of the officers had been sent from Stendal on the 17th of March by order of General Montbrun, that it never returned, but had been sent back to minister, and that they were in great need of their effects; the colonel also hoped that the general would have the regiment ordered immediately to join its division at the Grand Army. In a few days after, he received the order so much desired, for the regiment to join the 5th corps in all haste.

On the 15th of May they marched to Bernburg, and found the place occupied by Marshal Victor's army corps. On the 17th, they met General Puthod again at Dessau; he had orders also to join the 5th corps; so, the Irish regiment took its place again at the head of his division, and marched under his orders. They passed the Elbe at Wittenburg. General Puthod took Perry, the adjutant-major of the regiment, to be his *aide-de-camp*.

The division took the direction of Bautzen, always bivouacking at night. On the 20th of May they slept on the field amongst the dead, where General Lauriston had attacked General York the day before, and forced him to retreat. On the 21st of May, after marching several leagues, General Puthod's division, consisting of ten thousand men, arrived on the field of battle between Bautzen and Wurschen. The action had already begun on the whole line, and the 5th corps was completely engaged. General Lauriston was rejoiced to see his second division arrive at so important a moment; indeed, the arrival of these fresh troops contributed to decide the battle.

The general welcomed Colonel Lawless in the most friendly manner, and was delighted to see the regiment looking so well, after so much fatigue, and the fine band of music enchanted him, which, contrary to custom (at their own request), preceded the regiment until the battle began. But there was no time for compliments, the regiment was soon employed to attack the enemy, and after passing in close column over a part of the field of battle strewed with the dead and wounded, under a tremendous fire, Colonel Lawless deployed it and sent the grenadiers in front and the *voltigeurs* on the flanks to begin the attack, which proved successful, routing the enemy in every place, and at last, in the evening, taking the village of Wurschen, which gave the name of the battle of one of the two days' fighting.

The grenadiers of the Irish were pursuing the Cossacks through the court of the *château* of the village, when Marshal Ney arrived on horseback, and ordered the captain (Byrne, whom he recognised, having known him in Portugal during the retreat from Torres Novas) to halt there; he told him the battle was won, to remain on guard with him for the night, and to place sentinels to prevent the place being plundered. He brought the captain with him into the *château,* and as soon as he found a bedroom, he took a mattress, placed it on the floor, on which he flung himself down. He had his right foot swathed up in a napkin, having received a slight wound in it that day. He desired the captain to give the two sentinels at the door of the bedroom instructions not to allow any of his *aides-de-camp*, when they arrived, to disturb him if he happened to be asleep.

A colonel *aide-de-camp* who had followed the marshal, requested the captain of grenadiers to accompany him in examining the *château,* to see if the enemy had left provisions of any kind, and though every part seemed ransacked and destroyed, yet, by measuring and tracing, they found out a secret compartment in the cellar, in which were several hundred bottles of Tokay. The *aide-de-camp* apprised the marshal as soon as he was awake of what he had found, on which he ordered him to send for the generals that were in the neighbourhood to come and

BATTLE OF BAUTZEN, 1813

lodge there; he ordered also the captain of grenadiers of the Irish regiment to send to his colonel to come to the *château* to pass the night, and to send for the other company of grenadiers to be on guard, as they would be better there than at the bivouac.

Nothing could surpass his solicitude for the troops on this occasion. Generals Puthod, Vacherau and Pastol brought their provisions and accepted the marshal's kind invitation, as did Colonel Lawless and some other chiefs; but, except the wine, nothing was left in the *château*. As the headquarters of the Prussian and Russian armies had been there for two days, of course everything in the way of provisions was consumed. However, the generals and colonels, etc., spent a pleasant night in conversation on the glorious victory just gained; but all unfortunately were forced to own that the want of cavalry would prevent the great result that otherwise might have ensued; but for this the enemy's army would have been completely destroyed.

The orders for another general attack were given in the course of the night by the emperor for the ensuing day. Of course, all left the *château* before day, to repair to their respective posts, and Marshal Ney one of the first. He desired the captain commanding the two Irish companies of grenadiers to rejoin his regiment, which had bivouacked on the side of the road leading from Bautzen.

At about four o'clock in the morning of the 22nd of May, 1813, the emperor, who had passed the night on the field of battle a league off, arrived with all his staff officers, Marshal Mortier, etc. Marshal Ney, who had General Lauriston's corps under his orders, made the vanguard of the centre of the Grand Army, and Napoleon himself marched at the head with it to the attack.

During this day's manoeuvring and fighting, the Irish regiment was continually employed, and in the evening routed the enemy out of several villages on the road to Goërlitz, and only halted when night came on, at about a league from the town. This battle is called "*Combat de Reichenbach*"; in it the enemy had a vast number killed and wounded, and many taken prisoners. But Napoleon lost his friend and favourite, Duroc, Grand Marshal of the Palace. He was killed by his side late in the evening, as were two other generals of distinction, Lieutenant-General Bruyères and the General of Engineers, Kirgemer.

The stable in which Commandant Tennant had his horses took fire in the night, and they were extricated with much difficulty.

On the 23rd of May, the Irish regiment left General Puthod and joined the 3rd division of the 5th corps commanded by General Lagrange, to which it belonged. Having been detached on the Elbe, this was the first time they had joined the division, and they made part of General Suden's brigade.

The 23rd was spent in repairing the bridge over the Neisse, which had been damaged by the enemy, now in full retreat. After the three victories gained over them, they seemed resolved not to risk another battle, but from the want of old cavalry to pursue them, the infantry was continually employed attacking their rearguard

On the 24th of May the army arrived at Bunzlau, and had to wait till a bridge was thrown on trestles across the Bober, and then bivouacked on the other side.

On the 25th of May, the four divisions of the 5th corps making the vanguard arrived at Haynau early in the evening. The 1st division, commanded by General Maison, passed through the town and bivouacked at about half a mile on the other side. The three other divisions took a position before they came to the town. The 2nd division, commanded by General Puthod, to the right of the road leading to the town, and about half a mile; the 3rd, commanded by General Lagrange, to the left of the road, and the same distance from the town; the 4th division, commanded by General Rochambeau, at a certain distance behind the others.

All the dispositions to pass the night being taken, and several generals and colonels in the town, a sudden attack was made by about twenty thousand of the enemy's cavalry, who returned on General Maison's division, which suffered greatly from this unexpected charge, and would probably have been destroyed but for the 2nd and 3rd divisions, commanded by Generals Puthod and Lagrange, who marched immediately to their assistance.

The Irish regiment, fortunately, had nearly all its men present, as it only arrived the moment before the attack was made. Half an hour later, the men might have been all dispersed looking for provisions. The regiment formed a close column on the great road and marched on the enemy, and bivouacked on the field where General Maison's division had been attacked, or rather remained there all night under arms. The artillery of the 2nd and 3rd divisions soon stopped the enemy's progress. A Cossack officer being killed by the side of Colonel Lawless, he took the horse by the bridle and gave it to one of the officers (Captain Byrne) to carry his baggage.

When the Emperor Napoleon heard of the attack, and that the King of Prussia was with the army, he hastened to the advanced guard, and on the 26th, at daylight, after a very wet night, arrived at the bivouac of the Irish regiment, and ordered Colonel Lawless to form the hollow square, and designed the regiment to make the vanguard in this order with flying artillery on each flank. He sat on horseback at the head of the regiment for more than half an hour, viewing the plain, covered with the enemy's cavalry, and giving orders for the general attack.

General Lauriston, who expected to find the emperor greatly displeased with him, as well as with General Maison, on account of the disasters of the day before, told Colonel Lawless, with admiration, how Marshal Ney had, the moment he met the emperor, taken the whole blame on himself, by stating that every disposition was made after his orders and punctually executed. Of course, the emperor knew well how to appreciate this generous conduct; he replied, "Well, marshal, we must give them (the enemy) another lesson this day," and immediately the whole line marched forward to the attack, the Irish regiment in front, passing over hedges and ditches, and, as soon as they had crossed, forming again a hollow square, to be ready to receive the enemy should they venture to return to renew the charge. The *voltigeurs* of the Irish, as riflemen, were continually engaged driving the enemy's cavalry before them.

The emperor, during the whole day, was as much exposed as any of his generals, and several times they prayed him to remain behind, seeing the cannon balls passing over him like hail-stones. All were vicing at the same time who should be foremost in the danger. Marshal Ney and Generals Lauriston, Puthod and Lagrange showed the greatest activity with the advanced guards, giving orders everywhere that the enemy attempted to resist. It was a glorious day for the Irish regiment to have the honour of making the vanguard of such an army and under the eyes of Napoleon.

The enemy retreated through the town of Lignitz in great disorder. Captain Allen, at the head of his *voltigeurs*, entered the first into the town pursuing them. He was hailed by the emperor, who asked him to what regiment he belonged, and then ordered him to place sentinels at his lodgings, and to remain in town until he should be relieved by the Imperial Guards, who were following. The army bivouacked before Lignitz, and each division formed a hollow square, and passed the night in this order of battle.

During the day, an Irish sergeant of the name of Costello being reprimanded by Marshal Ney for not falling back immediately to the rallying place when the trumpet sounded, replied "that a Cossack had fired twice at him, and that he wanted to kill the fellow before quitting the field."

"And did you kill him?" asked the marshal.

"I hope so," said Costello, "for I saw him fall from his horse."

"*A la bonne heure!*" said the marshal.

The enemy fearing to risk another battle, and retreating rapidly, the French Army stopped in the same position before Lignitz the 27th and 28th of May, 1813, to repose and to give time to the other corps which were following to arrive. On the 29th of May, the army marched to Neumarkt, and rested there on the 30th; the 5th corps bivouacking near a windmill. It was here that General Lauriston told Colonel Lawless how pleased the emperor was with the regiment. He asked him if the officers of the battalions in Holland and at the depot were equally good with those present; if so, he thought they would be ordered to come and join the regiment in campaign.

On the 31st of May, the army marched on Lissa. General Puthod's division attacked the rearguard of the enemy. The General of Brigade Postell was killed in this affair. Lieutenant Osmond of the Irish regiment, who was doing the functions of *aide-de-camp* with General Vachereau, alighted from his horse, and was the first to march through the river under the enemy's fire, to encourage the men by his example. For this action he was much spoken of in the army, and was proposed in consequence of it for the cross of the Legion of Honour.

On the 1st of June, 1813, the army marched upon Breslau on the Oder. A deputation from the town came out to meet the army at some distance. The 5th corps passed by the town and bivouacked on the banks of the river. The enemy, instead of crossing the river, retreated up the left bank, in the direction of Schweidnitz; this movement made it be thought that they reckoned on the interference of Austria to obtain an armistice, which they eagerly sought.

In the night of the 1st of June, the 5th corps made a move from Breslau, and halted four leagues from it, when, in the morning following, news of the armistice was announced, and Colonel Lawless received orders to return to the camp before Breslau; in which place the regiment remained several days, until everything was finally arranged with the Russian and Prussian Armies respecting the armistice, which was signed on the 4th of June, 1813.

The armistice, or cessation of hostilities, was hailed with joy by the army; though they might be recommenced, it was consoling to be sure of having the prospect of real repose for a month, or perhaps two. I know that for myself, and all those who had made five campaigns in Spain without ever having heard the word armistice mentioned, it sounded like magic in our ears. I can never forget the night when Commandant Ware and I were sleeping at our bivouac, in a cornfield four leagues from Breslau, when *an aide-de-camp* came to tell him that an armistice was concluded, and that the regiment was ordered to return to its camp at Breslau.

In the morning, when I was awake, I began to say how sorry I was that my dream about the armistice was not true. Such was my state of exhaustion from want of sleep, that I did not know what to believe on the matter, though I was listening to the *aide-de-camp's* conversation with Commandant Ware. Next day, returning to Breslau, we found many of our soldiers still asleep on the roadside: this instance, with many others which I have experienced, proved to me that night marches should be avoided as much as possible.

During the stay at Breslau, the Postmaster of the Army arrived, and for the first time from the opening of the campaign the officers and soldiers received letters from their friends in France; but the baggage of the Irish officers was still behind. Many of them being in great need, made purchases at Breslau of linen for shirts, cloth for uniforms, etc. The cantonments being assigned to the different corps of the Grand Army, which they were to occupy as long as the armistice might last, each repaired to his destination.

The 5th corps, commanded by General Lauriston, had the neighbourhood of Goldberg; the 3rd division, commanded by General Lagrange, to which the Irish regiment belonged, left Breslau on the 6th of June, passed by Jauer, and arrived in a small village, Holberg, half a league from the town of Goldberg, where a camp for the division was traced, each regiment sending men to cut wood and bring it in to make huts. In a few days all were well lodged, and the camp of the Irish was much admired. Captains MacCarthy and Magrath left the regiment there, to be employed as *aides-de-camp* to General Casterolle, cousin of General Lauriston. Captain O'Reilly took the command of MacCarthy's company of grenadiers.

As soon as the four divisions of the 5th corps were properly encamped, General Lauriston reviewed them, and as the baggage of the Irish officers arrived the night before the review, they appeared to full advantage in their uniform and accoutrements, which had not been used during the three months' campaigning.

The six following officers of the Irish regiment were named knights of the Legion of Honour by the Emperor Napoleon on the 18th of June, 1813, and received their brevets at the camp at Goldberg: Commandant Tennant, Commandant Ware, Captain Byrne, Captain Saint-Leger, Captain Parrott, and Lieutenant Osmond.

Colonel Lawless went to headquarters at Dresden in the beginning of July, and obtained advancement for several officers and non-commissioned officers of his regiment. After he returned to the camp, he received cloth to make pantaloons for the soldiers.

The interval of the armistice was employed in exercising and manoeuvring the troops twice a day. The formation into hollow squares was particularly recommended to the regiments. From the want of cavalry, this order of battle became more urgent. The, soldiers were also employed digging entrenchments and filling them up, to accustom them to this kind of work, and every day something being done to embellish the camp, it soon became quite a nice little town. From being so near Goldberg, it was well supplied by the inhabitants with provisions, etc. The evenings were spent gaily, particularly on Sunday, when there was dancing and various amusements carried on with the people of the town and country and villages around.

During the month of July, a quantity of ball cartridges were distributed to each regiment that the soldiers might practise firing at the target.

At the end of July, General Lagrange's division being divided amongst the other divisions of the 5th corps, the Irish regiment returned to General Puthod's division and joined it at his camp about two leagues from Goldberg. They were glad to meet again those brave men with whom they had begun the campaign, and with whom they expected to share the dangers and honours of new combats, as the armistice was to cease on the 16th of August.

Napoleon's *fête*, which fell on the 15th of August, was celebrated by anticipation on the 10th of August, 1813, in order that they might have no chance of being surprised by the enemy in the midst of their festivities. As no expense was spared, and as the preparations began several days before, it proved splendid. General Puthod reviewed his division that morning, and made it perform various evolutions: manoeuvring in hollow squares, by echelons, firing blank cartridges, etc. Ten thousand soldiers and four hundred officers dined at the same table, and each man having his glass filled, drank to the health of the emperor, etc., the general giving the signal. In the evening the camp was illuminated, and many curious allegorical figures of victory, etc., with the emperor's effigy, were exhibited in transparent paintings. Between the dinner and the illuminations, there were races and other amusements.

Although the rejoicings at our camp, and everything in that way was cheering enough, and that the army had received, during the two months' armistice, reinforcements from France, still it was not encouraging to recommence hostilities with two additional powers against us; both Austria and Sweden had joined Russia and Prussia in the coalition with England against France. I well recollect the conversation which took place at General Puthod's table on the 14th of August, 1813, previous to the hostilities, on that subject. He said, as no two men ever hated each other as did Marshal Davoust and Marshal Bernadotte, the Prince of Sweden, "the war will be desperate if they are pitched against each other."

CHAPTER 8

Battle at Goldberg and Siege of Antwerp

Napoleon's splendid *fête* and rejoicings continued nearly all the night of the 16th of August. The five intervening days were busily employed, as everyone knew that hostilities were to begin on the 16th of August, and that Austria had joined Russia and Prussia against France. Marshal Macdonald, who commanded the 11th corps, had also the 5th corps commanded by Lauriston under his orders. According to the new dispositions, his army was to be opposed by Blücher and Langeron. The sick men were sent with the heavy baggage back on Torgau. On the 16th of August, General Puthod marched his division to the camp at Goldberg, and remained there on the 17th. On the 18th, before day, he left the camp and fell back on Lowenberg with his division, which was followed by the enemy's light cavalry, though not in great force.

There was skirmishing the whole of the way. The division arrived in the evening on the Bober near Lowenberg; the brigade to which the Irish regiment belonged, commanded by General Vachereau, bivouacked on the banks of the river, close by the town. General Puthod and the other brigade, with the artillery of his division, passed on the other side. On the 19th of August, at daylight, General Lauriston came to the bivouac and marched the brigade to an eminence about half a league from the town; he ordered the three regiments, 134th, 143rd, and the Irish, to be placed by echelons and to form the hollow square, with the Irish regiment in front.

These dispositions were scarcely effected, when he perceived the enemy's cavalry in great force, which rather surprised him, as he did not know that Blücher (contrary to the treaty of the armistice), had marched his army on the 14th of August to Breslau and Jauer, neutral towns which were not to be occupied until hostilities had recommenced.

General Lauriston immediately sent for Rochambeau's division, but before it had time to arrive, the enemy's cavalry charged the three hollow squares in the most furious manner. General Vacherau and his *aide-de-camp* came into the hollow square formed by the Irish regiment, which resisted the different charges made on it by the cavalry, who finding that they could not break it, brought a battery of artillery to bear on it, with grape shot and cannon balls, which no doubt made great havoc, carrying off whole ranks and files at every discharge; but the openings were instantly closed, and the cavalry, in spite of the aid of the artillery, were never able to break the hollow square, when General Lauriston sent *his aide-de-camp* to tell Colonel Lawless to endeavour to effect his retreat on a small wood and farmhouse half a mile in the rear.

The regiment executed this movement with the greatest coolness and bravery, observing the same order; the hollow square halting and firing every two minutes, until they reached the wood, which served to keep off the cavalry. General Rochambeau's division arrived on the field of battle with artillery and cavalry, and beat the enemy back two leagues.

The Irish regiment suffered much in this day's fighting. Three hundred men were killed and wounded. Four officers were killed, *viz.*: Commandant Tennant, Captain Evans, and Lieutenants Osmond and MacAuley. Eight officers were wounded, of whom Commandant Ware received three wounds and had his horse wounded under him. The others were Captains Parrott and Eckhart, Lieutenants O'Brien, Elliott, Brown, Wall and Peters. Colonel Lawless had his horse wounded under him in the hollow square. General Vacherau had his horse killed in the same hollow square, and would have been taken or killed had not Lieutenant Saint-Leger taken him in his arms and flung him over a wall into the farmyard, and had just time to follow him, when the cavalry arrived and sabred Lieutenant Elliott.

Commandant Tennant was cut completely in two; the cannon ball striking a belt in which he carried his money served as a knife to separate the body. The soldiers dug his grave with their bayonets, and when burying him found several pieces of gold that fell out of his entrails, and a part of his gold watch. Sergeant Costello, who was remarked on the 26th of May by Marshal Ney in the attack before Lignitz, lost his arm in this affair. The officers who escaped being wounded in this action had their uniforms bespattered with the blood and brains of the men killed beside them by the grapeshot from the enemy's artillery;

poor Tennant was giving orders to have the ranks closed and the gaps filled which had been opened by the artillery when he fell; his horse feeling he had lost his rider, dashed through the ranks and caused a still greater opening in the hollow square.

The Irish regiment returned and bivouacked that night, the 19th of August, 1813, on the same place it had been, on the riverside, on the night of the 18th.

On the morning of the 20th of August, a retrograde movement being ordered, General Puthod kept the Irish regiment in a village with himself about half a league from Lowenberg, the rest of his division bivouacking in the fields.

On the 21st of August, Colonel Lawless was ordered to hold his regiment in readiness to be reviewed by Napoleon, who was expected to arrive in the course of the day. Not meeting the Austrian Army at Zittau, on the side of Bohemia, the emperor made a rapid march to support Marshal Macdonald's army, and about one o'clock he arrived at Lowenberg. He immediately ordered a general attack; the Irish regiment had to pass through a mill, which stood in the centre of the river, the bridges having been destroyed the day before; the town was bombarded by the enemy's batteries. Under this tremendous fire, Colonel Lawless passed at the head of his regiment, and saluted the emperor, who was on horseback in the street leading to the river where the regiment had to pass.

The emperor was surrounded by his staff officers, the King of Naples (Murat), etc. Colonel Lawless seeing the grenadiers and the most part of the regiment had got through the mill, immediately rode through the river and placed himself at the head of his regiment to attack the enemy; he had hardly advanced a few steps, when his leg was carried off by a cannon ball from the enemy's battery, which was placed on an eminence to defend the passage of the river.

Colonel Lawless was brought into town upon a door by six grenadiers of his regiment. Napoleon saw him again as he returned wounded, and sent his chief surgeon, Baron Larrey, to perform the amputation, and afterwards sent one of his *aides-de-camp* to visit him, as did the King of Naples.

After Colonel Lawless was rendered unable to command, Commandant Ware had the command of the regiment, and Captains Byrne and Saint-Leger the command of the battalions as senior captains. The regiment continued at the head of the division in every attack on the enemy, till night put an end to the battle; they then remained in a village four leagues from Lowenberg.

General Puthod was so well pleased with it that he desired Commandant Ware, as soon as he should have leisure, to propose several officers for advancement, and to give him the demand, and that he should back it in such strong terms that the emperor would grant them immediately. As to Ware himself, he promised him he should be the colonel to replace Colonel Lawless; he saw Ware's wounds, and wanted him to stay in some place quietly until they were healed. Commandant Ware thanked him and said they would not prevent him going on horseback, and that he wished to continue to command the regiment Of course the general could not help admiring such resolution.

The army that marched with the emperor took no part in the action: his own presence sufficed, with Marshal Macdonald and Lauriston's two corps, about sixty thousand, to beat Blücher and Langeron, with a hundred thousand infantry and more than twenty thousand cavalry. General Maison was wounded this day.

The Imperial Guards and Marshal Marmont's corps of army bivouacked on the Bober near Lowenberg, and did not proceed further, but had to return on the 22nd in all haste with the emperor by Bautzen to Dresden, and arrived there on the 26th in time for the battle of that town.

On the 22nd of August, the 5th corps, commanded by General Lauriston, pursued the enemy's army, which, commanded by Blücher, was concentrated at Goldberg and prepared to give battle.

On the 23rd, at daylight, their outposts were attacked, and immediately after a general battle ensued on their whole line. General Puthod's division, with the Irish regiment in front, had orders to take the hill of Goldberg, on which the enemy's left wing was principally supported; this strong position was defended by the Russian infantry in the most brave and determined manner; the hill was twice mounted by the French, and twice were they repulsed; the third time General Puthod sent all his reserve, and the hill was taken after great slaughter, which might have been avoided had Rochambeau's division marched to turn the hill and left flank of the enemy; but that would have taken too much time, and the moral effect which the taking of this hill so suddenly produced on the whole line contributed considerably to the gaining of the battle, as the right wing and centre of the enemy's army, seeing their left wing forced to retreat, soon followed the example; besides, the French line advanced with such rapidity after the hill was taken, that the enemy could not resist. However, on account of the superiority of their cavalry, they effected their retreat in good order until night, as usual, put an end to it.

The Irish regiment lost some of its bravest soldiers, and had several officers wounded in this action. Captain Jackson in the heat of it was taken prisoner on the top of the hill and stripped nearly naked; his pocketbook, with his brevet and papers were found beside several dead bodies, which were naked and disfigured, with half their faces shot off. It was thought that Jackson was amongst them, and his comrades only knew the contrary a year after when he returned from the Russian prisons.

Commandant Ware had another horse killed under him at this battle. General Vacherau was killed in the beginning of the action, at the head of the Irish regiment, attacking the hill. Colonel Scibie and Colonel Aubert, both of General Puthod's division, received their brevets of generals of brigade on the hill during the battle. Colonel Aubert was wounded when he got his brevet.

General Scibie received the new colonel who was to replace him at the head of his regiment, and was immediately after received himself at the head of his brigade by Lieutenant-General Puthod.

After pursuing the enemy, a league from the field of battle, the division bivouacked in the plain. General Puthod kept the Irish regiment on guard with himself that night, and next day, the 24th of August, he proposed Commandant Ware for the rank of colonel, and Captains Byrne, Saint-Leger, Allen and O'Reilly for that of chiefs of battalion; he asked also eleven decorations of the Legion of Honour for the regiment, and the cross of officer of the Legion for Captain Parrott, who had already the decoration of Chevalier of the Legion of Honour. General Lauriston backed these demands in the strongest manner, and assured the regiment that the emperor would grant them immediately.

The division remained at this bivouac the 24th, where the melancholy ceremony of General Vacherau's funeral took place, a grave having been dug in the morning, and the brigade he commanded under arms, General Puthod made a very affecting speech, recapitulating all he knew respecting the military career of his brave comrade, under whom he had served as an adjutant sub-officer. He was the father of six children.

Marshal Macdonald knowing that Blücher had taken a very strong position at Jauer, took the necessary dispositions to dislodge him and to risk another general battle. On the 25th of August, his army began the movement forward, and on the 26th attacked the enemy's line with great success, until the heavy rains that fell during the action completely prevented the muskets going off, which gave the enemy, from the superiority of their cavalry, great advantage. General Puthod, who had orders to march into the mountains with his division to turn the enemy's left wing, met with the greatest obstacles in bringing up his artillery in consequence of the country being everywhere inundated.

On the 27th he heard of the disasters of Marshal Macdonald's army before Jauer and Katzbach. He immediately fell back on Hirschberg, where he found the Bober had overflowed the country for half a mile on each side, and with difficulty found a place to pass the night. On the 28th he continued his retrograde march towards Lowenberg, in which town he expected to rejoin the 5th corps.

He was followed by the enemy's cavalry and often attacked in front by them, but he forced them everywhere to fly before him, and lost very few in this day's skirmishing. Notwithstanding the bad roads and continual rains, the artillery was always up in time to attack whenever the enemy attempted to stop the road; but both horses and men were quite exhausted for want of rest and food. When the general got a favourable position, he bivouacked for the night at about two leagues from Lowenberg, and where he expected to get some news from Marshal Macdonald's army in the course of the night; but the only thing he heard was explosions of ammunition chests blown up, which indicated the distress of Macdonald's troops.

Early in the morning of the 29th of August, General Puthod marched his division to Lowenberg, having the Bober, which was overflowed, on his left. On his right was the enemy in great force. Seeing all the bridges carried away, and no possibility of constructing others, he took the best position he could near the town, to wait till the torrents had ceased rolling down from the mountains, or rather till they had in some measure abated, and there, with his division reduced to six thousand men, with 12 pieces of artillery, they defended themselves from eight o'clock in the morning till half-past four in the afternoon against more than forty thousand Russians and Prussians.

The Irish regiment during this action was continually engaged, and Captain Burke, who defended a village on the left flank of the division during the whole day in the most brilliant manner, and who received the highest praise from the general for his bravery, was killed at the close of the action with almost all the men under his orders.

BATTLE OF KATZBACH, 1813

General Puthod showed the greatest coolness and intrepidity in this critical and dangerous situation. The river in his rear increasing instead of diminishing, no prospect of assistance from the town of Lowenberg, where there were Westphalian troops that seemed occupied constructing a bridge; the enemy's army forming a complete half-moon round his division, each of their flanks joining the river, and no retreat possible, the general, in the centre of his division, fought until the last cartridge was fired, and even then, when the fire of his division ceased, the enemy hesitated an instant before venturing to advance. All of a sudden, at last, thirty thousand men ran forward on their prey, of whom none but those who knew how to swim could attempt to escape.

General Scibie, who was mounted on a superb charger, rode into the water, but the moment they got into the current both were drowned.

Commandant Ware's horse plunging and bringing him into the river, he flung himself from the saddle, and saved his life by swimming; the horse was drowned in an instant, as were all the other horses that reached the current.

Great numbers of men were drowned endeavouring to cross the torrent; however, about 150 of the division escaped. Eight officers and thirty men of the Irish regiment, with Commandant Ware and the ensign who saved the Eagle of the regiment, had the good fortune to get out of the bed of the river, but had to walk through a sheet of water which covered the other side for more than half a mile under the fire of the enemy, and many were wounded in this passage; had not the enemy been at this time in such disorder plundering the unfortunate prisoners, it would have been difficult for anyone to have escaped. The brave General Puthod and all his division, except those who escaped by swimming across the river, were taken prisoners and sent into Russia.

Norvins says (*Tome* IV):

D'un autre côté, la division Puthod, abandonnée seule dans les montagnes, après notre revers de la Katzbach, a succombé sous la supériorité du nombre, malgré une résistance héroique; et les flots du Bober ont enseveli tout ce qui n'a pu se sauver à la nage.

The River Bober at Lowenberg proved indeed a most unlucky place, for a part of the French Army at least and the Irish regiment had its share of the disasters on the 19th, 21st and 29th of August, 1813;

many were the sad and affecting scenes which occurred on those days. The person who writes these lines was present when the brave General Scibie asked his general of division, Puthod, if he would not endeavour to escape, getting for answer that it was impossible; "Well, I shall try, and risk anything sooner than go to Siberia;" on which he dashed into the water, and in a few minutes was no more. He was a splendid officer and a great loss. Six days only before, he got his brevet of General of Brigade, at the Battle of Goldberg, as is mentioned in a former page.

Captain Saint-Leger feared that his brother, Lieutenant Saint-Leger, had been one of the officers who fell at the advanced post, and indeed his fears and his sorrow were shared by all young Saint-Leger's comrades, for he was a great favourite amongst them. Captain Saint-Leger, however, bore up against his painful anxiety with the stoic fortitude worthy of a hero; but he could not bear up with the scene that ensued. He, Commandant Ware, and Captain Byrne, after their escape across the river, came to the street in the suburb leading to Laubau and Gorlitz, to wait to rally the men of the Irish regiment who might have crossed the river, when Lieutenant Lynch was seen coming along the street from the town. Commandant Ware asked him if there were any more still in the town.

"Yes," he replied, "but I could not get Saint-Leger to come with me till he got something to eat."

"What!" said poor Captain Saint-Leger, "my brother is not dead?" and, overwhelmed, he flung himself down on the ground, and was only relieved by a flood of tears.

Commandant Ware ordered Lynch to return, but Saint-Leger and a few men were soon perceived getting away from the howitzer shells that were falling about them.

This disaster, added to that of Katzbach, obtained for Blücher the title of prince.

Commandant Ware, with the few of the Irish regiment who escaped by swimming, marched to Laubau the same night, and on the 30th arrived at Goërlitz, where they were detained two or three days, to give time for the different divisions of Marshal Macdonald's army, which had been so much harassed for several days, to assemble.

The 3rd of September, the bridges were destroyed and the army retrograded. Commandant Ware, with the Eagle and the few who escaped, arrived at Bautzen on the 4th of September. Napoleon was then in the town with the Imperial Guards; he was on his way coming to the relief of his Silesian Army. He heard there of the fate of General Puthod's division, of which the Irish regiment made part. He was glad to see the Irish had once more saved their Eagle.

Commandant Ware waited on Prince Berthier, who ordered him, according to instructions from the emperor, to return with his detachment to the depot at Bois-le-Duc, and to collect the sick and wounded of the regiment in the hospitals who might be able to march. The Imperial Guards returning to Dresden, Commandant Ware marched along with them. But the town being crowded with troops, he marched two leagues further with his small detachment and slept in a village, after he had reviewed the field of battle where, on the 26th of August, 1813, so many thousands were slain.

This was the Battle of Dresden, where Napoleon, on the first day, the 26th, with sixty thousand men, and on the second day, with eighty thousand, beat Schwartzenberg with two hundred thousand men, and where General Moreau was killed.

Next day, Commandant Ware proceeded to Leipzig, where he intended passing the night with his detachment. Arriving on the *place d'armes*, he was informed that Colonel Lawless, with a number of the wounded men of the regiment, who had come from Torgau the day before, were on the point of setting out for Erfurth. Colonel Lawless being delighted to meet so many of the regiment alive after all the misfortunes of Silesia, preferred stopping an hour or two longer in town until the men of Commandant Ware's detachment had rested themselves. It was fortunate for him that he met Commandant Ware, for the detachment he was to have marched with was attacked on the road to Erfurth, about two leagues from Leipzig, and were nearly all taken prisoners by the partisans commanded by General Tillman.

Commandant Ware, with his detachment, got out as soon as the men were refreshed, and had made about half a league from Leipzig, when he met several retreating back who had escaped; he was obliged to return, and remained several days in the suburbs of Leipzig before he could venture to march, the roads being at this time nearly all intercepted by Cossacks and partisans. However, having recruited some wounded men of the Irish regiment who were able to march and fight, Commandant Ware proceeded by Mersebourg, Garbin and the Herz mountains, seldom knowing at night the road he should follow the next day, being obliged to wait to ascertain the direction not occupied by the enemy. Colonel Lawless suffered much in those bad roads, his carriage being often upset, and his wound opened in consequence.

After many days marching and counter-marching in those mountains, to avoid the enemy, Commandant Ware and his tittle detachment arrived safe at Paderborn, in which town he stopped two days to rest his men, and from thence to Munster, where General Harty commanded.

This brave officer entertained his countrymen in the most friendly manner, and thinking the country quite sure to the Rhine, invited Colonel Lawless, who was much exhausted by the journey, to stop with him a few days to recover. Colonel Lawless accepted, and the detachment marched to Wasal, but, the second day after, the Cossacks appeared before the town of Munster. Fortunately, General Harty had troops sufficient to drive them away, and Colonel Lawless escaped once more being made a prisoner.

He overtook Commandant Ware and his detachment at Cleves, and proceeded with them by Graves, and arrived at the depot of the Irish regiment at Bois-le-Duc in the beginning of October, 1813, after a campaign of eight months, in which the regiment had been continually employed in the vanguard and in the most dangerous and conspicuous situations, and frequently under the eyes of Napoleon himself; who mentioned to his Minister of War, Clarke, the Duke of Feltre, when he returned to Paris, how well the Irish regiment had served, and the duke told Colonel Lawless all this, and concluded, "This honour is all reflected upon me." ("*Tout ce que vous avez fait de bon rejaillit sur moi.*")

The officers of the depot, and Major Mahony who commanded it, entertained the small number of their comrades who arrived there after the disasters of this campaign with a dinner at Bois-le-Duc; but Colonel Lawless was too ill to be present at it: he needed rest to prepare him to undertake another journey. A few days after, he set out to join his wife and children at Paris, and to have his wound properly treated there.

When the Minister of War was apprised that Commandant Ware and the officers who escaped with him at Lowenberg on the Bober were arrived at the depot of their regiment at Bois-le-Duc, he immediately gave orders to have the first and 2nd battalions of the Irish regiment re-organised. Commandant Ware being then the senior *chef de bataillon*, got the command of the 1st battalion, which was soon completed with the men who were ready drilled and clothed at the depot.

Captain Byrne, by a decision of the Inspector of Wasal, was named

Battle of Hanau, October, 1813

to command the grenadiers of the 1st battalion, and Captain O'Reilly the grenadiers of the 2nd battalion. The latter obtained permission to go to Paris, and did not rejoin the regiment any more, being named, the following March, *chef de bataillon* in a French regiment.

Captain Allen was named to command the company of grenadiers in the 3rd battalion, and went to join it at Wilhelmstadt.

On the 2nd of November, 1813, Commandant Ware marched with the 1st battalion to Grave on the Meuse, to reinforce the garrison and to make head against the enemy then invading Holland under the orders of the Prussian General Bülow.

Some days after, Commandant Hayne and Lieutenants Saint-Leger and Brown were sent to Nimeguen, to be employed by Marshal Macdonald, who arrived there to command the troops on that part of the line. The month of November passed in slight skirmishing, and, at the end of the month, an order arriving for the regiment to be united at Antwerp, the 1st battalion returned to Bois-le-Duc, and from thence marched to Antwerp. The depot of the regiment being ordered to Lisle, on the 3rd of December the 3rd battalion, commanded by Commandant Dillon, evacuated Wilhelmstadt and joined the regiment at Antwerp, at which town the emperor ordered the four war battalions of the Irish regiment to be completed. Their conduct in the last campaign proved to Napoleon how he might count on these expatriated Irish in the hour of danger.

The Duke of Feltre named Major Mahony colonel of the regiment in the room of Colonel Lawless, who was to be named general at the next promotion. Lieutenants Ryan and Brelevet got the rank of captains, and several other promotions were obtained for non-commissioned officers and ensigns of the regiment. An order came at the same time to send away any Germans that might be in the regiment at Lisle, to be drafted into the company of pioneers. This order was no doubt given in consequence of the general disaffection of the various States of Germany to France in the last campaign.

Captains Saint-Colomb and Kenlan, with several men belonging to the 2nd foreign regiment (Isenberg), who had escaped from Italy, were sent to Antwerp to be incorporated into the Irish regiment. General Aubert, chief of the staff to General Maison, who commanded the first corps of army, took Captain Saint-Leger to be employed on the staff as one of the officers best suited for such a situation. Commandant Dillon left the regiment at Antwerp to be employed in the staff of General Maison, and did not return to it.

Battle of Hanau, October, 1813

The town of Breda being evacuated on the 12th December, 1813, Captain Byrne was sent with 500 men and six officers to the advanced posts at Braeschot, a small village on the great road to Breda from Antwerp, at which place he arrived on the 14th, late in the night. A company of engineers who were there cutting wood, and making fascines and gabions for the fortifications, had orders to return to Antwerp. The enemy had not as yet made their appearance, but Captain Byrne hearing that they had several thousand cavalry at their advanced posts, spent the night with his men barricading the village, and throwing great trees across the road where he had his outposts.

It was fortunate that he took these precautions and kept his men at bivouac all night round a great fire in the centre of the village, otherwise he could not have resisted, for at daylight the enemy's cavalry in great force attacked his advanced posts, which had orders to allow them to approach as near as possible before they fired; in the meantime he sent some men through a small wood to attack them in the rear, whilst he sallied out with the principal part of his detachment to attack them in front. He had succeeded in beating them back a league from the village when General Aubert, who commanded the 2nd division of the first corps at Merxicum, arrived to his assistance with a part of his division.

The general returned at night to his headquarters at Merxicum, and every morning he sent a reinforcement to Captain Byrne, who was continually engaged fighting the enemy's advanced posts, until he was relieved on the 20th of December by a battalion of the Imperial Young Guards.

Captain Byrne with his detachment made the vanguard of the division to escort a convoy of provisions to Bergen-op-Zoom, then partly blockaded by the English. He returned to Antwerp on the 28th of December, when he received great praise from the generals for his detachment, of which Sub-Lieutenant Esmond and Lieutenant Plunket made a part. Both these officers showed great bravery. On the 1st of January, 1814, Commandant Ware marched with the battalion to escort another large convoy to Bergen-op-Zoom with General Ambert, and had to skirmish with the enemy before the town until all got in safe.

This was the last detachment, the communication being completely intercepted: the English forces united to General Bülow drawing nearer to Antwerp. At this time General Decamp was replaced by the Duke of Plaisance, who commanded as governor. General Fauconet commanded the place. General Maison was commander-in-chief of the 1st corps. General Roguet and the Young Guards attacked the enemy's advanced posts, and had great success for several days.

On the 13th of January, 1814, the English, with a superior force, attacked Merxicum; General Ambert had to return under the cannon of the town. The Irish regiment had many killed and wounded this day. General Avey was killed in this action. The garrison remained under arms all night. Colonel Mahony was named this day to command an entrenched camp between the citadel and the town on the riverside.

On the 14th of January, 1814, at daylight, Commandant Ware, at the head of his battalion, retook Merxicum from the English, who retired on the road to Breda. He bivouacked with his battalion that night and returned next day to Antwerp, where he heard that the vacant place of "*gros-major*," or lieutenant-colonel, in the Irish regiment had been given by the Duke of Feltre to a Mr. Kenlan, the son of a Spanish general. He felt that he was bound, not only by what he owed to himself, but to the whole corps of Irish officers, to go to Paris to remonstrate with the Minister of War on the injustice of not leaving the advancement in the regiment to those officers who had so well merited it in the last campaign, and who had been so highly recommended to the emperor by Generals Lauriston and Puthod.

Unfortunately, these two generals were then prisoners of war. However, Ware, who had permission from the governor to go to Paris, succeeded with the Duke of Feltre (but not till the March following) in having Mr. Kenlan sent to some other regiment and he himself named instead to the rank of lieutenant-colonel, which left a vacancy of chief of battalion in the Irish regiment, to which place Captain Allen was promoted by a decree of the emperor in March, 1814.

After Commandant Ware's departure for Paris, Captain Byrne, as senior captain of the regiment, commanded the battalion; he was chosen at the same time by the governor to do the functions of superior officer for the visits, rounds, and all the other services of the place, which should come to his turn in that rank during the siege. Colonel Mahony being obliged to sleep in the entrenched camp, Commandant Hayne commanded the regiment in his absence.

General Maison, after leaving a garrison of about fourteen thousand men at Antwerp, retired with the rest of his *corps d'armée* by Louvain and Brussels.

In the end of January, Bernadotte, the Prince Royal of Sweden, who commanded a large body of Swedish and Prussian troops, marched upon Antwerp to complete the blockade of the town, with General Graham, who commanded the English forces.

Fortunately, General Carnot arrived on the 30th of January in time to complete the defence. A few hours after his arrival all communication between it and France was cut off. He immediately took the command as governor from the Duke of Plaisance. There was no time to be lost, as the English had already opened the trenches and were preparing to begin the bombardment. But Carnot's presence alone was equal to a reinforcement of troops; it both encouraged the soldiery and imposed on the immense population, which could not with safety be entrusted at this critical moment.

He soon proved by his genius and firmness that the town could resist for more than six months, and he accordingly desired that the inhabitants should make provisions for that length of time, or leave the town, whichever they liked best. A great many got the provisions necessary, others chose to leave the town and crossed the river. Several of the latter had sad reason to repent of the step they had taken, as they were plundered by the Cossacks encamped on the other side of the river, and they found no protection from those pretended liberators.

The day after General Carnot's arrival the English commenced bombarding the town. He saw they had attacked the weakest part of the fortifications, but he soon had a battery of 36-pounders and several mortars erected on the rampart. On that part, by the aid of thousands of the inhabitants whom he put in requisition to make small sacks and fill them with clay and carry them to the rampart, the parapets of the battery were all constructed during the night.

On the 1st of February, 1814, the English, no doubt, must have been surprised to find from this weak point, as they thought, a battery of 12 pieces of 36-pounders, and four great mortars, playing on their works, which prevented them advancing; but they continued to bombard the town, and particularly the quarter where the French fleet was laid up in the basin, without, however, damaging the ships of war, as the sailors kept the ice which surrounded the ships continually broken, and had the decks covered with several feet of dung and clay to prevent the shells injuring them.

General Carnot seemed quite in his element having so important a place to defend, and he gained new vigour according as the danger increased. Having brought only one *aide-de-camp* with him from Paris, he took four officers of the Irish regiment to be employed on his staff during the siege: Lieutenant Saint-Leger, who spoke French, German and English perfectly well, was one of those in whom the governor placed most confidence. It was he who was entrusted to go to the advanced posts and to receive the enemy's flag of truce whenever they had anything to communicate to the governor, and to bring them into the town when required, blindfolded, according to the precautions taken in time of war on such occasions. Lieutenant Saint-Leger evinced the greatest activity and bravery during the siege, for which the governor proposed him to the Minister of War for advancement.

When the communication with France became completely intercepted, General Carnot wished to ascertain if he could raise money from the merchants, bankers and other rich inhabitants of Antwerp to pay the troops. They refused to make any advancement, though he offered them, as a guarantee for the payment, all the copper of the arsenal, to the amount of several millions of *francs*. He was then obliged to get money made of the copper, which he called "siege money" (*monnaie obsidionale*), with which the soldiers were paid, and as this coin contained more weight than the intrinsic value, it passed readily through the town. But General Carnot intended to try other means to raise money, and not to waste the copper which was so necessary in the construction of the ships.

He had an old Dutch ship of the line filled with stones lying in the river, which he intended sending down near Lillo, to have her sunk in the narrow part of the river the moment an English fleet should attempt to sail up. This alarmed the commercial interest; and to add to that, he had three of the principal bankers arrested and put on board this ship, which was to serve as their prison. But the wives of these gentlemen soon waited on the governor to know what was to be done to get their husbands liberated. He showed them a list of a hundred of the richest inhabitants of the town, and asked them if they thought the gentlemen whose names were there inscribed could afford to lend him three thousand *francs* each, for that was all he wanted. They exclaimed they could, and ten times as much, and offered to take the list and get it signed, on which he immediately gave orders for their husbands to be put at liberty.

After this transaction, General Carnot became a great favourite at Antwerp. He invited the authorities to assist him in organising a city guard, or *garde urbaine*, which was immediately executed and composed of the most respectable inhabitants. They rendered the greatest service, as they furnished guards and patrols every night with the troops of the garrison, and by this means the best order was observed during the different sorties which were made against the enemy.

On the 6th of February, the governor took advantage of a sudden thaw to order a sortie to be made on the enemy's entrenchments, which they were forced to abandon in disorder, and they retired in the direction of Bergen-op-Zoom.

Prince Bernadotte wrote to General Carnot inviting him to give up the town and join, what he termed, the good cause. The governor answered him, he thought it ill became a French prince, who owed all his greatness to the valour of the French Army, to invite one of its generals, to whom reputation and honour were dearer and of more value than aught beside, to dishonour himself and become a traitor.

Carnot published this correspondence in the daily newspapers of Antwerp, and at the same time ordered a sortie to be made to attack the advanced posts of Bernadotte's army, in order to prove to him how much he despised his offer.

Whilst General Carnot was the terror of the enemy without, he acted with the greatest humanity towards the inhabitants of the town; he preserved an entire outlet, or village, or suburb, which the commissioner of engineers thought necessary to have razed for the defence of the place. These poor people were so grateful that they gave the name of "Rue Carnot" to their principal street, and had the name put up in gold letters.

The English General Grahame, after he had been obliged to suspend his attack on Antwerp, was encouraged by the offer of some of the inhabitants of Bergen-op-Zoom to attempt to surprise the weak garrison of that town. Accordingly, on the night of the 8th of March, 1814, from three to four thousand English troops were conducted by a Dutch retired captain who lived there through a subterraneous passage, and got possession of almost all the batteries on the ramparts before midnight, meeting with hardly any resistance.

But General Bighany soon assembled his little garrison of young conscripts, and before twelve the next day (the 9th), and after great slaughter, the English were obliged to lay down their arms, and instead of opening the gates of the town, as they expected, to let in their general, had to surrender themselves prisoners of war.

Two officers, one French, the other English, were dispatched to Antwerp to have the capitulation confirmed by the governor, Carnot; General Bighany being under his orders, this formality was necessary. The English prisoners gave their parole that they would not serve against France during the war; so, they were set at liberty, and sailed for America soon after.

The news of this victory had the best effect on the garrison of Antwerp, which was greatly reduced a few days after—General Maison being obliged to manoeuvre and open the communication with Antwerp on the French side, in order to bring General Roguet's division, composed of about six or seven thousand Young Guards, to reinforce his army corps. The Irish regiment saw this brave division quitting the town at so critical a moment with regret, as the service of the place became harder; but the governor inspired such confidence that everyone knew he would find means to supply the division that marched away with General Maison.

He immediately ordered that all the military workmen belonging to the arsenal, and all the French *employés*, of every description, should be armed and clothed with the uniforms of the different magazines of the hospitals to the number of six or seven thousand; and at the general review on the Sunday following, the inhabitants (who thought that from the garrison being lately so much reduced it could not resist much longer), were quite at a loss to know how so many fine men could be armed and disciplined in so short a time; they were made to know that every Frenchman is a soldier.

By this last measure, General Carnot proved to the people of Antwerp, as well as to the enemy without, that his resources for the defence of the town were far from being exhausted, and the more he learned of the reverses in France, the more he was decided to hold out to the last extremity; for Paris, as an open town, might be taken and retaken without deciding the war one way or another, and he determined in no case to believe anything coming from the enemy's quarter.

However, on the 1st of April, he assembled the council of defence, composed of the *prefet*, the admiral commanding the fleet, the generals, etc., and they agreed that the chiefs of the different regiments composing the garrison should be sent for, to ascertain from them the spirit of the troops, or, in other words, if they could be counted on to defend the town to the last. All these chiefs answered for their soldiers, saying that nothing could exceed the bold, determined spirit which animated them.

In consequence of some correspondence of Colonel Mahony's being intercepted, he was put under forced arrest on leaving the council, and the command of the Irish regiment given to Commandant Hayne. General Carnot knew well that Mahony was a French emigrant that had served in England.

On the 10th of April, 1814, a courier from Paris was allowed to pass the enemy's line and to enter Antwerp with the intelligence respecting the events which took place in the capital on the 31st of March, and the subsequent abdication of Napoleon.

The governor fearing to be the dupe of any deception, and wishing to have accurate information on so important a subject, despatched an officer to Lisle to ascertain from General Maison the truth, and all the particulars relative to the change of government.

As soon as the officer returned, General Carnot signed an armistice with the English General Grahame. The hostilities ceased, but the service of the outposts was more strictly executed than ever, and the governor took the greatest precautions to preserve to France this important fortress, with its military stores, arsenals, dockyards, immense fleet, etc.

On the 18th of April, another courier from the Minister of War, General Dupont, arrived at Antwerp with positive orders to proclaim Louis XVIII.

The next day, the 19th of April, 1814, the governor and all the troops of the garrison took the white cockade and declared for Louis XVIII.

Colonel Mahony's arrest being raised before this ceremony took place, he resumed the command of the Irish regiment.

Commandant Allen received his brevet as chief of battalion (which had been detained at the depot of the regiment at Lisle by Lieutenant-Colonel Ware, who had been waiting for the communication with Antwerp to be opened).

General Carnot permitted a few English officers to come into town, but they were obliged to be in coloured clothes, to avoid any disputes with the garrison.

The final instruction to evacuate and surrender Antwerp to the English having arrived, the governor, Carnot, on the 2nd of May passed the Scheldt with the first division, and the brave garrison of Bergen-op-Zoom evacuated that town; immediately after, the English Army marched in and took possession of it.

Thus finished the memorable defence of Antwerp, which began in December, 1813, and ended on the 4th of May, 1814, where the governor, General Carnot, displayed the genius of a Vauban, the inventive resources and tenacity of a Hannibal, with the honesty and modesty of a Cincinnatus.

★★★★★★★★★

On the melancholy occasion of the death of Mr. Byrne in January, 1862, Mrs. Byrne received a letter from Colonel d'Esmond, who had made his first campaign as a *sous*-lieutenant under Mr. Byrne at the siege of Antwerp in 1814, in which there is the following passage:

"*Madame—Veuillez agréer l'expressoin de ma reconnaissance pour votre bienveillant souvenir, au moment de vos souffrances et de la perte de monsieur votre mari, mon brave et vaillant compatriote et frére d'armes. En 1814, il dût la vie à la croix de la Legion d'honneur centre laquelle vint s'amortir une balle et je n'oublierai jamais le sangfroid avec lequel, lorsque je ramassai et lui prèsentai le projectile, le héros me donna des ordres!*"

★★★★★★★★★★

CHAPTER 9

Napoleon's Return

The Irish regiment marched from Antwerp to Dunkirk on the 4th of May, 1814, by Ghent and Bruges. Colonel Mahony left the command with Commandant Hayne and went himself to Paris, to see the Minister of War, General Dupont.

The regiment stopped a few days at Dunkirk, to pay and settle with the Polish soldiers that belonged to it, and then had them sent to Saint-Denis, near Paris, where the Emperor Alexander was assembling all the Poles that were in the French service, in order to send them back to their own country.

The corps of Irish officers paid a visit at Dunkirk to their countryman, General F. O'Meara, who had so bravely defended Dunkirk against the English under the Duke of York in 1793.

The Irish regiment marched from Dunkirk to Lisle to join the depot commanded by Lieutenant-Colonel Ware, and arrived there on the 16th of May, 1814. General Gazan, who had just come as inspector-general, told the officers of the regiments born in France that they could choose, if they wished, a French regiment, in which they would be placed to concur in the new organisation of the army. A few who were not on good terms with Colonel Mahony availed themselves of this offer, *viz.*, Captain Brelevet, Lieutenants Marshal, Saulard, Tumoral, Lagrange, Kerthin, etc. Colonel Mahony returned from Paris and rejoined the regiment at Lisle. He was then decorated with the Turkish Order of the Crescent, and signed himself "Chevalier de Mahony," in the orders he gave to the regiment.

Captain Nugent, the son of an Irishman, but born in France, having drawn for money on a house at Paris that did not exist, had to leave the regiment after a decision of all the captains, his comrades, who declared him unworthy to serve with them after such a transaction. In a fit of drunkenness, he committed an act which brought disgrace on his respectable family; and though he had squandered a handsome property left to him by his father, still his pay as a captain ought to have sufficed for him, as it did to his comrades. He was a fine, well-looking man, more than six feet high, brave, and well-informed.

After a lapse of more than sixteen years, Lieutenant-Colonel Ware was agreeably surprised to receive at Lisle a visit from his friend and old comrade, William Aylmer; they had been chiefs of the insurgents during the war of 1798, in the county of Kildare. Their plans not succeeding, they were obliged to separate. Aylmer went to Austria, and got a commission in the army of that country. Hugh Ware was detained in the prison of Kilmainham, at Dublin, till the Peace of Amiens, 1802, in violation of the treaty he had signed to expatriate himself for ever from the British dominions.

Aylmer had the rank of captain of cavalry in the Austrian service, and he was on his way to London, by the orders of the Emperor of Austria, to conduct and present in his name to the Prince Regent a Husard soldier and horse, completely equipped and caparisoned, to serve as models for the English cavalry. Captain Aylmer's mission obtained for him the Prince Regent's pardon, and leave to return to his native country, Ireland, where he remained with his family and friends till he joined General Devereux at Dublin in recruiting and organising a legion for the Spanish South American independence.

As soon as the 1st battalion was completed, he sailed with it, and rendered much service, both morally and physically, before he received the wound of which he died. Had he survived, he would have been rewarded by the President Bolivar and the government of that country for which he fought so valiantly. How melancholy it is to think of such brave men not having a country of their own to fight for!

On the 24th of June, 1814, the Irish regiment left Lisle and marched to Avesnes, where it arrived on the 28th of the same month, and where it was expected the re-organisation of it would soon take place; but it was still undecided whether the French Government would keep Irish regiments in its service; besides, the officers who had had the misfortune to be taken prisoners in the last campaign were not all yet returned to the depot; several arrived during the month of July from the Russian prisons, and others were on their way back.

On the 3rd of August, the Duke of Berry arrived at Avesnes; he was accompanied by Marshal Mortier. They breakfasted at the *sous-prefec-ture*, and after breakfast the duke received Colonel Mahony, "Chevalier de Saint-Louis." He set off immediately and did not review, the troops of the garrison that were waiting under arms on the place. He gave permission to the colonel to allow the officers to wear the *fleur-de-lys*. On the 4th of August, Lieutenant-General Burke arrived at Avesnes as inspector-general, to re-organise the regiment, but it appeared he had not as yet his final instructions to begin, so everything remained in suspense. The general, however, after inspecting the regiment, encouraged the officers and assured them of his solicitude for their welfare.

On the 25th of August, 1814, the *fête* of Saint-Louis, the king's birthday, the corps of officers gave a dinner to the general and the authorities at Avesnes, and a ball and supper in the evening at the theatre, which was splendidly decorated for the occasion. Unfortunately, at the opening of the ball, Colonel Mahony insulted Captain Lawless with the grossest language and then ordered him away under arrest.

On Lieutenant-Colonel Ware, however, observing to the colonel that on a day of rejoicing like that they were then celebrating, it would be better if it passed over without having anyone punished, he consented to raise the captain's arrest, and to allow him to remain at the ball, for which Lieutenant-Colonel Ware thanked him; but in less than fifteen minutes after, on Colonel Mahony meeting Captain Lawless, he again insulted him worse than before, and ordered him to quit the room immediately. Lieutenant-Colonel Ware wishing to remonstrate, the moment he spoke, Colonel Mahony ordered him also under arrest.

Upon which Lieutenant-Colonel Ware said to him: "I will go home and guard my arrest, but I must tell you, before I go, that your conduct this evening is unworthy of a gentleman, and it is both cowardly and scoundrelly of you to insult an officer like Captain Lawless, whom you know cannot bring you out."

Colonel Mahony went to the box where General Burke was looking on at the dance, to inform him no doubt of what had taken place, and that he had put the lieutenant-colonel under arrest, etc. The ball became rather dull in consequence of this unpleasant affair, for almost all the Irish officers went away when they heard of Colonel Mahony's insolent conduct. The general could not approve of it, but he did not wish to say so publicly.

The next morning, the 26th of August, Lieutenant-Colonel Ware received a note, stating that his arrest was raised; he immediately waited on Colonel Mahony to know with what arms he wished to fight, and said, that for his part, sword or pistol were equal. They fought with pistols, and after exchanging shots, Mahony and his second seeming satisfied, left the ground, though Lieutenant-Colonel Ware refused to make any apology for what he had said the night before. Commandant Allen and Captain Parrott were the seconds to Lieutenant-Colonel Ware. Captain de Tressan and a French colonel, who had married Miss Magrath, a cousin of Mahony's, acted as seconds to him.

The Sunday after this duel, when the corps of officers with Colonel Mahony at their head, waited on General Burke, he railed in the most violent manner against Lieutenant-Colonel Ware for having had the audacity to speak as he did to his colonel the night of the ball, adding he deserved to be tried by a court-martial. This speech surprised the officers, as they knew well that the general was acquainted with all the circumstances of the duel and of Colonel Mahony's conduct on the occasion, and they thought all had been forgotten.

From that moment the Irish officers could perceive a preference shown to the Prussian officers whose regiment had been disbanded in Holland in 1813 by order of Napoleon. After the Restoration, all these German officers were sent to be incorporated in the Irish regiment, and two captains of them, of the name of Geitz, received their brevets as chiefs of battalion from the Minister of War, Dupont. These, with the great number of German captains ordered to be comprised in the new organisation of the regiment, left little or no hopes to the brave Irish officers of obtaining the advancement they had so well merited in the last campaigns of 1813 and 1814 (as well as for their former services), and for which they had been so strongly recommended by Generals Lauriston, Puthod, and Carnot Many had to serve in the same rank eight or ten years more before they could get promotion; Lieutenants Saint-Leger, O'Brien, Swanton, etc., were of this number.

On the 10th of September, 1814, the depots of the 1st and 2nd foreign regiments, Latour-d'Auvergne and Isenberg, with a great number of officers arrived at Avesnes. General Burke was charged to organise these two regiments also, but he had still to wait for instructions till the month of December, when the skeletons of the three regiments were ordered to Montreuil-sur-Mer, where they were definitively organised by General Burke, as 1st, 2nd, and 3rd foreign regiments in the French service, leaving out the former appellation of *3rd régiment étranger irlandais*. It was said at the time that Lord Castlereagh required this omission of the word "Irish," and objected to the re-organisation of the Irish brigades, which he supposed the government of the Bourbons might wish to see re-established, as they were before the revolution of 1789.

The 1st and 2nd regiments marched to the south and south-east of France as soon as they were re-organised. The 3rd regiment (*ci-devant troisième régiment étranger irlandais*), in which the Irish were comprised, remained at Montreuil-sur-Mer. It was organised into three battalions and a depot, in which all the Irish officers not comprised in it were placed and allowed to follow the regiment until places became vacant in it for them. As these officers could not be sent to their homes, they were to have the same pay, and to do garrison duty with the other officers of the regiment.

The following are the names of the superior officers composing the 3rd foreign regiment *ci-devant irlandais.*

Mahony, Colonel.
Ware, Lieutenant-Colonel.
Braune, *Chef-de-Bataillon.*
Hayne, *do.*
Allen, *do.*
Geitz, *do.*

The battalions were very weak, but as the regiment was allowed to recruit on the frontiers, it was expected they would soon be completed. Besides, the vast number of discharged soldiers were generally ready to re-enter the service. The non-commissioned officers were a very good class of men, and much attached to their officers, with whom they had served in the last campaigns; they could not see with satisfaction other officers put to command them.

Captain Parrott, who commanded a company of grenadiers during the siege of Antwerp, and who had distinguished himself in so many campaigns, particularly in that of Silesia, where he was wounded and proposed for the cross of officer of the Legion of Honour on the field of battle, saw his company of grenadiers given to Captain Saint-Colomb, who came from the regiment of Isenberg, and who had never commanded a grenadiers' company. But the latter pleased the colonel and General Burke, who was charged with the organisation of the regiment. This was one of the many instances of injustice which the Irish officers had to submit to after the Restoration, and Captain Saint-Colomb felt it himself, for he waited on the general, accompanied by Captain Parrott, to request him to name Captain Parrott to the grenadiers' company in his place, Parrott having the best right to it. The general was enraged to hear of such a proposition, and would not undo what he had done.

Colonel Mahony having got the regiment organised (as he thought) to his liking, obtained permission to go to Paris in February, 1815, where he intended to marry Miss Power, the daughter of one of his comrades in the old Irish brigade; but the marriage articles not being ready when Napoleon landed, Mahony, like every other officer on leave of absence at that time, was obliged to return to his regiment, and the ceremony of the marriage was postponed.

Commandant Hayne, who thought he was advantageously known to the Inspector-General Burke for many years before, got his retreat without being consulted, which was a crying injustice, as he would have been entitled to the maximum the year after. He was in perfect health and fit for service; but he had the misfortune, as a member of the council of administration, not to agree with Colonel Mahony about the accounts of the regiment. There could be no just reason for treating so worthy a man as Hayne in so brutal a manner as to send him, after 29 years' honourable service and so many campaigns, to live on a pension of fourteen hundred *francs* a year, and to deprive him obtaining the cross of the Legion of Honour, which he prized above rank or anything.

An Irishman being thus treated, whilst the Prussian officers whose regiment was disbanded by Napoleon in Holland, in 1813, were kept in activity, showed that the Irish had little to expect from the government of the Bourbons, and made them fear subsequently that Lord Castlereagh's influence would become so great as to require that no Irish should be kept in the French service.

Colonel Mahony returned to Montreuil-sur-Mer on the 15th of March, 1815, and retook the command of his regiment, and in the first order of the day that he gave he signed himself "Count O'Mahony." This was the first intelligence the officers had of his being a count.

As the newspapers from Paris arrived regularly every day at Montreuil-sur-Mer, Napoleon's rapid march on Paris was no secret. Napoleon arrived at Paris on the 20th of March, 1815.

The Irish officers, as men of honour, knew what they owed to themselves, and that as foreigners they should not meddle in the change of government, but serve faithfully the one established until they were absolved from their oath of allegiance. Under this impression, they exerted themselves for several days to keep the non-commissioned officers and soldiers in order, which at such a crisis was no easy matter, as all knew that the emperor was at Paris. Colonel Tobin, who commanded the town, and who knew the Irish regiment at Antwerp, asked for Commandant Allen and his battalion to be lodged in the citadel with him. Every precaution was taken to observe the best discipline and order.

On the 25th of March, 1815, Colonel Mahony assembled all the officers of the regiment at his lodgings, apparently to consult with them on the events which had taken place at Paris. He mentioned that the King, Louis XVIII., was on his way to Lisle, and he wished to ascertain what the officers thought on the subject. Lieutenant-Colonel Ware replied:

"Colonel, give your orders, and they will be executed. If the king wants an escort to the frontiers, he may rely on the regiment doing its duty. But we Irish patriots will never go to the enemy's camp to fight against France, our adopted country."

Colonel Mahony rejoined: "For his part, he was decided to follow his king, which he considered '*le chemin de l'honneur.*'" Besides, he added, he could not think of ever again serving the emperor after what had taken place at Antwerp during the siege of 1814, when he was under the orders of General Carnot. He therefore was resolved to go off that same day. He then gave up the command of the regiment to Lieutenant-Colonel Ware, sending him the military chest, etc.

After Colonel Mahony's departure, Lieutenant-Colonel Ware and the corps of officers determined to wait for orders from the general commanding the military division at Lisle before they should change the cockade; and in consequence the troops were consigned to their quarters to prevent any collision with the inhabitants of the town, many of whom had already put up the three-coloured cockade.

Early next morning, the 26th of March, the *sous-préfet* and civil authorities received orders from the prefect of the department to declare for the emperor; but the military instructions for the garrison, transmitted by Marshal Mortier, did not arrive till some hours later. On receiving this order, by which all the military were absolved from their oath of allegiance to Louis XVIII, all the troops of the garrison under arms, with the National Guards and civil authorities, repaired to the *place d'armes*, where the Emperor Napoleon was proclaimed with the greatest expressions of satisfaction and joy.

The Irish regiment on this occasion displayed the Eagle which they had so often defended from the enemy, and which had remained in the military chest of the regiment during the eleven months of the Restoration, and which was now brought out.

The greatest harmony and good understanding existed between

the inhabitants and the troops on this important ceremony. Lieutenant-Colonel Ware thought proper to tell such of the officers of the regiment who might have any scruple in serving Napoleon, that they were at perfect liberty to retire. Three only availed themselves of this permission and went away, *viz*.: Captain de Bonan, Captain Ferguson, and Lieutenant Gordon. All the other officers swore allegiance to the Emperor Napoleon, and signed an address expressing their devotion to him and his dynasty.

Colonel Mahony returned next morning, the 27th of March, and told Lieutenant-Colonel Ware that he had come back to resume the command of his regiment, and ordered him to send the Eagle and military chest to his lodgings. To which Lieutenant-Colonel Ware replied: He would never serve under him, nor acknowledge him for his colonel; consequently, he had no orders to receive from him; that he was astonished to see him so mean after his fine declaration on the 25th in presence of the whole corps of officers; or that he could suppose that men of honour could overlook his conduct.

Colonel Mahony then applied to the governor of the town, Colonel Tobin, who immediately sent for Lieutenant-Colonel Ware and ordered him to execute the orders of Colonel Mahony, who, he said, had returned to take the command of his regiment, and to serve the emperor faithfully. To this Lieutenant-Colonel Ware answered, no power on earth should oblige him to serve under the orders of a traitor. He then deposited his sword with Colonel Tobin and considered himself under arrest. All the officers of the regiment, without one exception, went individually to Colonel Tobin's lodgings, and there deposited their swords, declaring they would never take them back to serve under Mahony. Captain Magrath, Colonel Mahony's first cousin, deposited his sword like the other officers, and seemed to disapprove of Mahony's conduct as much as any of them.

The governor finding he could get no officer to execute his orders, went himself and brought a detachment of grenadiers from the barracks of the Irish regiment and escorted the Eagle and military chest to Colonel Mahony's lodgings, which was considered very unwise of him; it incensed the officers more and more to see their Eagle intrusted to a man they thought unworthy of commanding them. The same evening, the 27th of March, General Pellet, who arrived at Montreuil-sur-Mer, assembled all the officers of the Irish regiment; he begged of them to take back their swords and to continue to serve under Colonel Mahony until the emperor should decide on the question; but to this they all replied, no power on earth would oblige them to serve one instant under his orders.

Finding it useless to persevere further with, men so determined as the Irish officers were, the general told Mahony what he had to expect; the latter, therefore, determined a second time to follow "*le chemin de l'honneur*," but this last time it was to Paris he went, instead of following his king to Ghent; and it was feared, that through General Burke's influence with Marshal Davoust, then Minister of War for Napoleon, that Colonel Mahony might be sent back to the Irish regiment. But, fortunately for these brave men, General Carnot was also at that time one of Napoleon's ministers, and of course he told him of all Mahony's treasonable conduct at Antwerp, so there was nothing more to be dreaded on that subject.

Lieutenant-Colonel Ware and the other officers, though unarmed, used all their exertions to keep the troops consigned, and as soon as Mahony left the town, the general invited them to retake their swords and to continue to serve as before.

Thus, this change of government finished quietly, and to the great satisfaction of the Irish officers, who saw with much joy the influence of England, with that of Lord Castlereagh, cease in France. They now felt assured that their former campaigns and services would be recompensed by the emperor.

Colonel Tobin, who appeared so anxious to have Mahony reinstated, in spite of the Irish officers, was soon replaced himself in the command of the town. On the 6th of April, 1815, Colonel Peltier took the command as governor, which situation he had before the Restoration, under the emperor. Residing at Montreuil-sur-Mer, and being there during the late events, he was able to appreciate the conduct of the Irish regiment on that important occasion. He had also the advantage of being known personally to the emperor of a long date, as one of the representatives of the people who accompanied General Buonaparte in Paris on the 13th *vendémiaire* (5th October, 1795), when the latter dispersed the sections which were marching to attack the Convention and the Government.

Colonel Peltier had under him, to command the place, Commandant Gallibert; the latter wanted an arm; he had been a long time employed at Genoa, before it was evacuated by the French. The artillery was commanded by the Chef-de-bataillon Pillault, who had been in the service of King Joachim (Murat), and returned to France in 1814. The greatest harmony and friendship existed between all these brave officers and the Irish regiment.

Commandant Hayne, who had been so unjustly treated in the month of March, being in Paris when the emperor arrived, claimed, and was reinstated in the Irish regiment with his rank as before. He remained in Paris with permission, and did not return to the regiment till after the second Restoration.

Captain Parrott, who had been so unjustly treated by the Inspector-General Burke, got his company of grenadiers, which had been given to Captain Saint-Colomb; the latter, to do him justice, never wished to retain it, and he requested Lieutenant-Colonel Ware to give the company to Captain Parrott, who, he added, had the best right to it.

In the beginning of May, 1815, Lieutenant-Colonel Ware received his brevet from the emperor as colonel of the Irish regiment, which caused great pleasure to all the Irish, and even the German officers seemed to be as much pleased at his advancement as the Irish officers themselves could be; in short, he was loved and esteemed by everyone who served under his orders, and deservedly, for he was brave and ready to promote the interest of all.

By another decree the emperor allowed the regiment to resume its former number and name of *premier régiment irlandais*, which greatly gratified the Irish officers, as they hoped, by this last act, that Napoleon had once more turned his thoughts towards their oppressed country, and that the day might not be far distant when they should be sent on an expedition to Ireland, where their military experience would powerfully contribute to throw off the English yoke under which their country had been suffering, and been degraded for centuries.

The Minister of War, Marshal Davoust, wrote by command of Napoleon to Colonel Ware on this occasion a letter which contained the most flattering expressions for the Irish regiment. The emperor declared that he would hereafter employ it in every circumstance and with the same confidence as he would employ one of the imperial regiments of his Guards. The greatest union and emulation subsisted in the regiment during the month of May, and soldiers were arriving daily to complete the four battalions which composed it on the war establishment. Several officers who were on half pay were sent to be attached to the regiment, and two Spanish officers who were on half pay were allowed to join it, *viz*.: Captain Garido and Lieutenant Ferarie. Captain Murray had been retired and lived at Dunkirk; he rejoined his old comrades with pleasure.

The commander of the artillery Pillault invited all the officers of the Irish regiment who were not employed in the instruction of the troops to follow with him the exercise of the artillery, which they accepted with much eagerness; and this brave commander saw with pleasure the rapid progress which they were making, passing four hours every day on the ramparts at the manoeuvres of the artillery.

In the beginning of June, the Governor of Montreuil-sur-Mer received instructions from the Minister of War, informing him that it was ascertained that the English Government, in the event of hostilities beginning on the frontiers, intended landing five or six thousand men on the coast, to make a diversion in the rear of the French Army; that the emperor thought the Irish regiment, with the national guards of the country, would be quite sufficient to destroy and disperse the expedition as soon as it landed.

Napoleon judged well, for though the Irish regiment had not yet had time to have all the battalions completed to the war establishment, the good spirit with which the officers and men were animated, and the good understanding which subsisted between them and the National Guards, was a sure guarantee of success.

The prospect of being actively employed in this way against the English consoled the Irish regiment for not making part of the French Army in the Low Countries, where they had hoped they might have had another opportunity of proving their attachment to their adopted country, and their devotion and gratitude to Napoleon for the confidence which he honoured them with.

One of the emperor's *aides-de-camp*, Lieutenant-General Dejean, who arrived at Montreuil-sur-Mer at this time, met there several of the Irish officers who served under his orders in Spain, at the advanced posts, when the English Army was driven into Portugal in September, 1811, at Fontelgenalgo, Alfitas, etc., and, by meeting these officers, General Dejean was enabled to appreciate the good composition of the Irish regiment, of which he made a most favourable report to Napoleon when he returned to Paris.

Soon after his departure, two emigrant captains of the regiment, Magrath and Saint-Colomb, though they had sworn allegiance to the emperor, began to correspond with the enemy at Ghent. Captain Saint-Colomb deserted on the 10th of June, 1815, and was followed two days after by Captain Thompson. The latter was born in France and had served in the Prussian regiment before he joined the Irish regiment. Though these officers were Frenchmen, yet the indignation of the Irish was not the less.

In consequence, eight captains of the regiment waited on Captain Magrath and reproached him with his infamous and dishonourable conduct. He could not deny that he corresponded with the Bourbon party at Ghent, nor that he had accompanied Captain Saint-Colomb on the road the day he deserted. The eight captains told Magrath that they were resolved not to serve with traitors, and said he must resign. They also informed Captain de La Roche, another French emigrant, that he was accused of corresponding with the enemy. Fortunately, the Irish officers were not answerable for the dishonourable conduct of men who broke that allegiance to which they had sworn voluntarily.

Napoleon having joined the army in Flanders, and news arriving of his having gained the Battle of Fleurus on the 16th of June, in so splendid a manner, the highest hopes were excited in the hearts of the expatriated Irish. Their feelings on this occasion cannot be described. They imagined they were once more on the point of making part of an expedition to liberate their unfortunate country from the cruel tyranny of the English Government. But the loss of the Battle of Waterloo on the 18th of June, with the other unhappy circumstances which followed Napoleon's abdication, put an end to their career, and to all further hopes of aid from France to relieve Ireland from her bondage.

The *sous-préfet* of Montreuil-sur-Mer received instructions from the provisional government of Paris to proclaim Napoleon II, consequently all the civil authorities and the officers of the garrison were assembled at the municipality to swear allegiance to him. The sensation this ceremony created was very great, and gave a temporary hope that the nation might rally once more to drive out the enemy. About the same time an order from the Minister of War arrived at Montreuil-sur-Mer for the Irish regiment to march immediately to join the army in the neighbourhood of Paris; but Colonel Peltier, who commanded the town and district, and who received the order, did not think proper to communicate it to the commander of the regiment, Colonel Ware, wishing, no doubt, to keep the troops in the garrison to be ready to proclaim Louis XVIII, when he should have orders for that purpose from Paris.

Accordingly, on the 11th of July, 1815, the order arrived, and Louis XVIII was proclaimed a second time on the 12th of July, 1815. It was on the arrival of this last order that Lieutenant Thulier, being on guard, and going up to the top of the rampart to speak to the courier before admitting him into the town, lost his balance, fell over and was killed on the spot.

The Marquis de Bryas, who had been at Ghent with the king, arrived at Montreuil-sur-Mer and took the command from Colonel Peltier as governor of the district. The same day several of the Irish officers, with Colonel Ware at their head, expressed to him their hesitation at continuing in the service under so many changes. This gentleman very properly observed to them that they should not rashly sacrifice their claims upon France, their adopted country, where they had served with so much distinction, having always done their duty as men of honour, and having executed punctually the orders of their chiefs. They might regret the sudden changes, he said, but they were not answerable for them. If anything could lessen the pain of their position, seeing an English Army in possession of Paris, and their own prospects so changed, it was the friendly reception the Irish officers met with from the Marquis de Bryas whilst they remained at Montreuil.

Colonel Ware drew up an address on the 13th of July to be forwarded to the king through the Minister of War. It was left at the quartermaster's to be signed by all the officers of the regiment. Commandant Braune, a Prussian, and several of his countrymen, though they signed it, assembled immediately afterwards at his house and got Lieutenant Wall, the son of an Irishman, to draw up another address, in stronger terms, in which they styled themselves the "true and real royalists" of the regiment.

This second address became, of course, a kind of denunciation against those officers who did not sign it, and a sure recommendation in favour of all those who put their names to it, as they were soon after employed, and even several were placed in the Royal Guards. Those officers who had complied strictly with their colonel's orders were marked out for persecution. Such was the encouragement given to insubordination at that melancholy period, that the very worst officers were sure of employment and advancement, provided they boasted of their devotion to the Bourbons and spoke against their comrades.

Several disputes took place between the Irish officers and those Prussian officers who had been put into the regiment after the Restoration. Captains Jackson and Town had duels with two of those Prussians, and wounded them dangerously. The Marquis de Bryas fortunately listened to Colonel Ware's advice and put an end to all this by refusing to receive any further denunciations of these Germans against the Irish.

On the 15th of July, the Marquis de Bryas having heard that a battalion of National Guards from Rouen, which had been stationed at Dunkirk, and were returning to Rouen to be disbanded there, were still wearing the tri-coloured cockade, marching across the country, called on the Irish regiment, with two pieces of artillery, to go and meet them. On arriving at Hesdin, the marquis met them coming in by small detachments, having taken out their cockades. About thirty or forty kept with their commander and made their way into Normandy. The next day the Marquis de Bryas returned with the Irish regiment from Hesdin, bringing his wife with him to Montreuil, she having been staying at their residence at Hesdin. They gave some agreeable entertainments at Montreuil, of which place he gave up the command in September, 1815.

By this time the army of the Loire being completely disbanded, the Irish regiment could not expect to be better treated than those brave and unfortunate men. General Desnoyers was sent in quality of inspector-general; he was assisted by M. le Pautre, *sous-inspecteur aux revenus*, and on the 28th of September, 1815, at Montreuil-sur-Mer, they finished their painful task of disbanding the Irish regiment that had served in all the campaigns of Germany, Spain, Portugal, etc., from 1803 down to the present date, 1815, for twelve years of continued campaigns, without interruption; often and deservedly receiving the highest encomiums from the different generals-in-chief under whose orders they served during these memorable campaigns.

According to the inspector-general's instructions, the officers were to choose and name the towns where they wished to retire to on half pay: consequently, they were soon dispersed all over France. The sergeants, corporals and private soldiers of the regiment who wished to remain in the French service were marched off to be incorporated in the Legion of Prince Hohenlohe, then forming at Toulon. Captain Town took the command of this detachment, and set out on the 29th September, 1815. Colonel Ware, Captains Byrne and O'Vitzky, as members of the council of administration of the regiment, and Lieutenant Wagner, quartermaster, and Lieutenant Montague charged with the clothing, received orders from the Minister of War, Clarke, Duke of Feltre, to remain at Montreuil in order to terminate, sign and give up the different accounts of the regiment, and also to have the military effects remaining in the magazine of the corps forwarded to the Hohenlohe legion.

Particular instructions were given on this occasion to Lieutenant

Montague to have the "N." eagles, and all other signs bearing allusion to the emperor, effaced from the effects before they were sent off.

Two beautiful standards were sent to Spain by the emperor in 1810 for the 2nd and 3rd battalions of the Irish regiment, but they were left at Valladolid, as those battalions were then in Portugal. These standards were brought to the depot of the regiment and were destroyed by Lieutenant Montague at Montreuil. They were green with a large harp in the centre. On one side in gold letters "Napoleon I. to the 2nd Irish battalion." And on the other "The independence of Ireland." The 3rd the same. The Eagle was carried by the 1st battalion, which, of course, had its colours like the others.

The officers of the council left at Montreuil received two-thirds of their pay until the February following, and when all was finished, they retired on half pay like the other officers, hoping at least to remain unmolested. But soon after the Battle of Waterloo the brave regiment was disbanded by Louis XVIII, and the Irish officers were made to feel that Lord Castlereagh and English influence prevailed in the French councils.

Commandant Allen, who had retired to Melun, was ordered from that town to Rouen, and passing by Paris, was there arrested by order of the Duke of Feltre, and informed he must quit the French territory without delay. Thus, without trial or judgment, one of those officers whose gallant actions had gained such renown for the Irish regiment, both in Spain and Silesia, was to be banished from his adopted country by the orders of General Clarke, the son of an Irishman.

Lieutenant-General Arthur O'Connor waited on the Duke of Feltre and insisted that Commandant Allen should be brought to trial, saying, "It was too bad to see him worse treated here than he had been when tried and acquitted with him at Maidstone." The duke, knowing well that no charge whatever could be brought against Mr. Allen before a court-martial, had no idea of having him tried, but seeing that General O'Connor took up the matter so warmly, and fearing no doubt that he might have it published in the English and Irish newspapers, after much hesitation, consented to have Allen set at liberty, and allowed him to retire to Tours on half pay, where he remained a prisoner at large until 1830.

Captain Jackson was also banished by order of the Duke of Feltre, without any trial or charge whatever being brought against him; and yet this brave officer had distinguished himself on every occasion where the regiment had been engaged, either in Spain or Germany.

He was wounded and taken prisoner at the Battle of Goldberg in Silesia on the 23rd of August, 1813, and had only returned from the Russian prisons of Siberia a few days before the emperor's return from Elba. Captain Jackson sailed from Havre in November, 1815, for South America, where he had a further opportunity of showing his military talents fighting for the independence of that country.

Captain Town, a brave and most distinguished officer, full of information and learning, and military genius, was, like Jackson, banished by the order of the Duke of Feltre, without trial or appeal to any military tribunal a sad recompense for all his gallant services! He being in the neighbourhood of Marseilles, sailed for Italy, where he found great difficulty in being allowed to remain.

Another victim, still more remarkable, of the Duke of Feltre's vindictive feeling towards the Irish regiment was Captain Lawless, who was ordered to quit France forthwith, although he was personally and advantageously known to him, having been for more than two years attached to his staff in Paris, in 1812 and 1813. Notwithstanding this, and all the influence and exertions of his uncle, General Lawless, he could not obtain the favour of a trial by a court-martial, which, indeed, would at once have put him at liberty, as no charge whatever could have been brought against him.

He was obliged to leave France, and went to New York. General Lawless must have felt this most keenly, when he recollected the many flattering letters, he received from the Duke of Feltre respecting the brilliant services rendered by the Irish regiment in Germany, at Flushing, etc., saying "He gloried in them as an Irishman!"

This system of persecution appeared the more extraordinary, from the colonel, Ware, being exempted, who should have been the first to incur blame, if any could be attached to the corps. On this occasion, it is only justice to Colonel Ware to say that he gave in to the Minister of War a very long and detailed report after the regiment was disbanded, specifying every occurrence that took place during the Hundred Days, and for which he himself, as "*chef de corps*," felt he was alone responsible.

Having related the brutal treatment which Commandant Allen, Captains Lawless, Jackson and Town received from the Duke of Feltre, I ought to mention my own, which was still worse, on account of the time allowed to intervene before it was perpetrated. They received the order to quit France in 1815, and I only received it on the 2nd of January, 1817, the order to quit Tours in twenty-four hours, and France in fifteen days. Whether this postponement was on account of my being one of the members of the council of administration charged with rendering finally the accounts of the regiment, or for other motives, I never could learn; yet it was well known at the War Office that the ministerial decision was taken against me at the same time as that against Captain Allen and the other officers. As to my sufferings, and the way I obtained justice, they would be too long to insert in a note.